THE FREEDMEN'S SAVINGS BANK

THE FREEDMEN'S SAVINGS BANK

A Chapter in the Economic History of the Negro Race

By WALTER L. FLEMING, Ph.D.

PROFESSOR OF HISTORY IN
VANDERBILT UNIVERSITY

NEGRO UNIVERSITIES PRESS

WESTPORT, CONNECTICUT

Originally published in 1927
by University of North Carolina Press, Chapel Hill
Oxford University Press, London

Reprinted in 1970 by
Negro Universities Press
A Division of Greenwood Press, Inc.
Westport, Connecticut

SBN 8371-3590-7

Printed in United States of America

PREFATORY NOTE

This account of the Freedmen's Savings Bank is an expansion of a paper prepared in 1905 for the December meeting of the American Historical Association and published in the YALE REVIEW *in 1906. I am indebted to the editors of the* YALE REVIEW *for permission to use the substance of that article.*

CONTENTS

THE FREEDMEN'S SAVINGS BANK

THE FREEDMEN'S SAVINGS BANK

Chapter I

THE NEGRO AT THE CLOSE OF THE CIVIL WAR

THE Freedmen's Savings and Trust Company, commonly called the Freedmen's Savings Bank or the Freedmen's Bank, was a result of the efforts of the northern friends of the Negro to find a means of elevating the newly emancipated race which would train its members in habits of thrift and economy, and which, by encouraging them to save their earnings, would aid them in securing a stronger economic position in the social order. The organization in 1865 of the Freedmen's Bank system was one of the few sensible attempts made at the close of the Civil War to assist the ex-slaves, who had been brought very suddenly face to face with freedom and its responsibilities. It was a promising plan for the elevation of an almost helpless people, and its failure caused serious injury to them at the time and continued to be felt for a long period. The purpose of this account is to outline the history of the organiza-

1

tion, to describe its possibilities, its development,
its decline and collapse, and to show how it in-
fluenced the Negroes.

ECONOMIC WEAKNESS OF THE NEGRO RACE

Aside from the question of race and status perhaps the greatest weakness of the Negro population in 1865 was its extreme poverty. In spite of
destruction by war there was still much accumulated wealth in the southern states, but it was
in the hands of the stronger race; the Negro,
therefore, could not begin with equal opportunities. Under slavery the Negro had assimilated
much of the white man's civilization: he could
speak the language; he had accepted the Christian religion; and in manners and customs he had
imitated the whites. But slavery, though it had
eradicated many primitive traits and had shown
the Negro what he had not previously known, the
virtue of hard labor, still had not taught him
self-reliance or thrift. So the year 1865 saw the
Negro population of the United States, with
what it had gained during the period of servi-
tude, thrown suddenly into a somewhat highly
organized, though defective, economic society,
with some serious weaknesses to hinder its well-
being and progress. It was an alien race in America; it was not self-reliant; it was not experienced;
it was uneducated; and it had almost no economic asset except its capacity for labor.

The Negro's ability to work was then, and has
been at all times since then, the greatest strength
of the race. In the South this labor was much
needed, and there was a possibility that within

a reasonably short time many individuals might attain economic independence. Wages were high after the war; the cost of living was not great in the South and the Negro's expenses for the necessities of life were not heavy; land was a "drug on the market" and could be purchased for a mere fraction of its former value. If the weaknesses of the Negro could be strengthened, if he could at once take advantage of the opportunities offered, his place in the social organization would be better assured.

GRADUAL EMANCIPATION

What was the actual condition of the Negro population when "Freedom cried out"? An examination of the conditions surrounding the race during the latter years of the war and in 1865 will lead to a better understanding of the economic difficulties that it had to solve, and will help to a better appreciation of the possibilities of the Freedmen's Bank system. It must be remembered that, although the mass of the Negroes was not free until after the surrender of the Confederate armies, large numbers of them had before that time passed through a transition stage toward freedom. In North and South in 1860 there were half a million free Negroes, many of whom had acquired property. The Federal army, as it invaded the South, gave practical freedom to many thousand slaves in the border states and in the theatres of war. During the first year of war these "contrabands," as they were frequently called, were employed as laborers in the Federal camps and on the military

works. As compensation they were given subsistence only.

The next step toward freedom and experience
was the admission of Negroes to military service.
The Washington government rather reluctantly
at first armed a few black regiments for garrison
duty, but allowed them no pay. The individual
northern states then began to send small numbers into the army as substitutes who were paid
as state troops. After much effort on the part of
the friends of the race the United States government in 1863 enrolled Negro regiments, which
were regularly armed, uniformed, and officered.
But the pay, fixed at $10 a month only, was still
unequal to that of white soldiers, and no bounties
were given. Not until toward the close of the
war were Negro troops placed upon an equal
footing with the white forces. The Negro soldiers, numbering more than 200,000 in all, were
recruited partly in the northern states but
mainly in those districts of the South which were
reached in 1863–1864 by the invading Federal
armies. These Negro soldiers and the laborers in
the camps, with their families, probably num-
bered more than a million persons who, slaves
in 1861, were free and to a certain extent trained
and experienced before the downfall of the
Confederacy.

Slavery as a labor system was early destroyed
by the mere friction of war in the border states
of Missouri, Kentucky, West Virginia, Maryland, and Delaware, and in large sections of
Virginia, Tennessee, and Arkansas. Where the
Federal forces came into a community it was

there impossible to hold the slaves at work, for they could leave home easily and go to the free states or follow the armies. So in the border states or near the military frontier, the master who would control his labor at all was obliged to give his slaves what was practically a free status. While the effect of the war in these regions was mainly to disorganize the slave system and to demoralize the workers, the latter had nevertheless by 1865 made some progress toward looking out for themselves.

NEGRO LABOR UNDER FEDERAL SUPERVISION

The occupation by the Union armies of large districts in the South affected thousands of slaves in addition to those who were enlisted in the Union army. Their masters, if Confederate sympathizers, were driven from home; the country was laid waste by the contending armies; and the responsibility for the care of the slaves left behind was thus thrown upon the Federal commanders. At first the homeless, masterless people were neglected; later they were allowed to form refugee camps near large military posts and scanty rations were doled out to them. But their numbers increased so rapidly, their sufferings were so great, and their presence was so embarrassing to the movement of the Federal forces, that each principal commander organized for his army or for his district a sort of "Department of Negro Affairs" to take charge of the slaves who were captured or who came within the Federal lines as refugees.

General Benjamin F. Butler, at Fortress Monroe in 1861, set the example of confiscating captive slaves and organizing them to work for their own support. When Port Royal was captured by the Federals in 1862 the Negroes of the Sea Islands were organized under agents sent from the North by the United States Treasury Department. For three years, under a system resembling benevolent serfdom, these agents trained the Negroes for the responsibilities of freedom. And elsewhere along the Atlantic coast where the Federals secured a hold, colonies of refugees were thus organized to work for their own living. The lands, houses, and movable property of the Confederates were used for the benefit of the refugee slaves who, by the end of the war, had begun to work without supervision and in some cases had purchased property.

A similar policy was pursued by the commanders in the Southwest. After the fall of Vicksburg and Port Hudson the Negroes near the Mississippi River from Cairo, Illinois, to New Orleans passed under the control of the Federal armies, whose commanders, in order to lessen suffering and prevent starvation, gathered them into camps or colonies near the military garrisons. Officers of the army, usually chaplains, were detailed to look after Negro affairs, to collect the homeless ones into these colonies, to provide for the distribution of supplies and for medical attention to the sick. General Grant had begun this policy in 1862 when he set all the Negroes near his army in West Tennessee to picking cotton and gathering corn in the deserted fields. Chaplain John Eaton supervised this work and in 1863 was placed in charge of all the Negro camps and colonies in the Mississippi valley above Louisiana.[1]

Though there was more than enough work for all, there was strong rivalry between the War Department and the Treasury Department over control of "Negro affairs." In 1863 and 1864 the Treasury Department leased to private speculators the abandoned Mississippi valley plantations in the districts controlled by the Federal forces. The Negroes were then required to work for the lessees, who in return furnished them with subsistence and paid or promised to pay them wages. But neither Eaton's colonies nor the Treasury plantations were successful. In the camps and on the plantations the neglected Negroes died by thousands from want and disease. When the crops failed, the laborers received no return for their work, and even when good crops were made, the lessees frequently swindled them out of their wages.

An interesting experiment with Negro labor was tried in lower Louisiana from 1862 to 1865. General Butler and his successor, General Banks, maintained a "Free Labor Bureau," which was charged with the supervision of labor on the plantations of the Confederates who were away at war, and with the regulation of the relations between the Negroes and those masters who remained at home. The result here, just as on the Atlantic coast and in other parts of the Mississippi valley, was a sort of temporary serfdom. The Negro was forced to work, while the Federal

[1] Eaton, *Grant, Lincoln and the Freedmen, passim.*

authorities saw that he received food, clothing, and sometimes wages. Regular contracts were made and enforced when possible by the army officers. The speculators and planters made little money; in fact most of them lost heavily, but the Negroes secured some training for the responsibilities of freedom.

Such were the conditions surrounding the Negroes who escaped from slavery before 1865. The camps, colonies, and settlements, whether on the Atlantic coast or in the border states, or in the Mississippi valley and along the Gulf coast, were constantly receiving accessions of escaping slaves. These came through the lines, or were brought out by such expeditions into the interior as that of Banks up the Red River valley or Sherman's raid to Jackson, Mississippi, or his march through Georgia. All of those thus freed from slavery had some experience and training before the general emancipation.

But the majority of the slaves remained with their masters until very nearly the end of the war. They worked as usual or better than usual on the plantations where, because of the absence of so many of the white men, more than ordinary responsibility was thrown upon them. In the Confederate armies numbers of them were employed as teamsters and as laborers on fortifications and in the munition factories. The slaves within the Confederate lines were better cared for and had better health than those in the camps and colonies within the Federal lines, but at the time of emancipation they were probably less fitted for the responsibilities of freedom.

Thus, at the close of the war, all the Negroes were somewhat better prepared for freedom than they were in 1861: the slaves on the plantation by the increased opportunities given during the war for the development of self-reliance and independence of character; the Negro soldiers by their experience in army life; and the Negroes in the colonies and on the abandoned plantations by their sufferings, by having to rely upon themselves, and by their familiarity with the customs of free and half free labor; and all of them by the partial throwing-off of servile habits.

DEMORALIZATION AT THE CLOSE OF THE WAR

Conditions following the surrender of the Confederate armies and the consequent general emancipation were not favorable for the well-being of the Negroes. Nearly 200,000 Negro soldiers, somewhat unfitted by army life for peaceful pursuits, were gradually mustered out of service with no homes to go to and with several hundred thousand of their relatives scattered over the border states and in the camps and Negro colonies. To unite families was difficult and often impossible. The abandoned plantations were soon given back to the white owners, a proceeding which unsettled the Negroes who had expected a division of property. The refugee colonies were disbanded one by one, throwing numbers of blacks into the world with no plans and with hardly any faculty for making plans. Many of those who had remained slaves until 1865 now attached themselves to the armies of occupation or crowded around the garrison posts.

That they would never have to work any more, never be hungry or cold again, was the belief of many of those last emancipated. These were also possessed by the general idea that in order to be really free they must leave their old homes for new ones and must take new names. Men frequently deserted their families and took on new "free" wives. Thousands wandered over the country living from hand to mouth—eating berries, green corn from the fields, and stolen chickens and pigs. In the crowded cabins near the towns and the military posts want and disease, often epidemic, thinned the numbers of the Negroes until it was estimated that the blacks had lost by death as heavily as did the southern whites during the war. For several years after the war the death rate among the Negroes in the cities was twice as large as that of the whites. J. D. B. DeBow[2] stated in 1867 that the laborers had decreased twenty-five per cent in number since 1860, an estimate certainly too large except for the congested camps and colonies.

The system of labor based on slavery was of necessity disorganized as a result of emancipation. In May and June, 1865, industry was, as far as the Negroes were concerned, almost at a standstill. Those who were congregated in the towns and about the garrisons could find little to do, and those still in the country were too excited over their new freedom to work regularly. Latham, an English traveler who went through the South in 1866, said that the Negroes had secured old muskets and had become "a race of

[2]Editor of DeBow's *Review.*

hunters." Crops were poor in 1865 and again in 1866, and the white planters and farmers were so reduced in means that they were unable to pay cash wages to Negroes. It was several years before a workable labor system was evolved.

In addition to the freedmen's general roving there was a stream of migration from the Atlantic states toward the Southwest, while all over the southern country there was a constant moving toward their old homes of thousands who had been carried by their masters into the interior to escape capture by the Federals, and of those who had enlisted in the Federal armies or had followed them out of the South, or had been gathered into the numerous "contraband" and refugee colonies. Frederick Douglass thus described conditions: "The government had left the freedman in a bad condition. . . . It felt that it had done enough for him. It had made him free, and henceforth he must work his own way in the world. Yet he had none of the conditions of self-preservation or self-protection. . . . He was free from the individual master but the slave of society. He had neither money, property, nor friends. He was free from the old plantation but he had nothing but the dusty road under his feet. He was free from the old quarter that once gave him shelter, but a slave to the rains of summer and to the frosts of winter. He was turned loose naked, hungry and destitute."[3]

"FORTY ACRES AND A MULE"

The "Forty Acres and a Mule" delusion exer-

[3] *Life and Times of Frederick Douglass*, by himself. I, p. 89.

cised an unsettling influence for several years. The Negroes had reason for believing that the government would give them land with which to begin the free life. The use of Confederate property for the Negroes during and soon after the war, the widespread discussion of confiscatory measures, and especially the action of General Sherman in dividing up the Sea Islands and the Georgia and South Carolina coasts among those who had followed the army, caused the fieedmen to entertain the fixed belief that each family was to get "forty acres and a mule." This pleasing idea, fostered to a considerable extent by the subordinates of the Freedmen's Bureau, kept many from settling down to regular work, and prepared the way for swindlers who for years made a business of selling fraudulent titles to lands to thousands of Negroes.[4]

FAILURE OF NORTHERN PLANTERS

Another blow to the prospects of the Negro was the general failure of the northern planters who came south during and immediately after the war expecting to make fortunes by raising cotton, rice, and sugar cane. The native planters had little or no capital, and plantation equipment and supplies were lacking. The free Negro distrusted the southern white, who in turn had little confidence in free Negro labor. Land was cheap, and a southern planter was glad to secure a northern partner or to sell his land to a northern capitalist. It was also thought that the Negro would work better for a northern em-

[4] *North American Review*, Vol. 182, p. 721.

ployer or manager. The prospects, therefore, seemed good for the northern man who had some capital. But nearly all ventures by the northerners were unsuccessful for numerous reasons. The newcomers were ignorant of planting methods; their trust in the Negro was sometimes reckless and caused them to lose heavily; frequently they endeavored to exact more efficient work than the Negro could give and thus gained the dislike of the latter; and after a year or two politics became such a disturbing factor that crops were neglected. The failure of the northern planters made northern capital more unfriendly, the southern planters gradually went to ruin, and the resulting depression injured the Negro.

THE FREEDMEN'S BUREAU

During the fall and winter of 1865–1866 nearly all of the southern legislatures enacted laws later known as the "Black Codes" which were designed to check the roving and thieving propensities of the Negroes and to hold them to work and to a settled abode. This legislation so strengthened the already existing northern distrust of the southern whites that, by means of the Freedmen's Bureau and the military forces, the Negroes were removed entirely from local legal control, and the southerners were prevented from directing their economic progress. The irritation and disagreement resulting caused severe disturbance of economic conditions.

The Freedmen's Bureau, created in 1865 by a Congress distrustful of the southern master

class, grew out of the various "departments of
Negro affairs" and other attempts that had been
made during the war to regulate the life and
work of the Negroes who had come under Federal control. The Bureau, designed to act somewhat as a guardian for the race, was by the
beginning of 1866 organized in all the former
slave states. It was administered in the War
Department at Washington by a Commissioner-
General, O. O. Howard, under whom in each
state there was an assistant commissioner with
numerous district superintendents, local agents,
inspectors, school superintendents, and teachers.
The confiscated Confederate property, public
and private, was turned over to the Bureau
which continued to administer the numerous
refugee colonies for the year 1865 and then disbanded them. The institution, by aiding in the
support of missionaries and teachers, engaged
extensively in church work and education. Contracts had first to be approved by the official of
the Bureau who had supervision over all matters
relating to Negro labor, such as contracts, time,
wages, and treatment. The subordinates who
were in immediate control of the Negroes were
usually ignorant of local economic conditions
and frequently were corrupt and arbitrary; their
activities aroused false hopes among the Negroes, unsettled industry, and prevented the early
working out of a free labor system. The relief
work of the Bureau lasted for more than two
years and in some sections resulted in considerable demoralization.[5]

[5] For Freedmen's Bureau Acts, see Fleming, *Doc. History of Recon.*,
I, p. 319 and Peirce, *Freedmen's Bureau, passim.*

Charitable societies and individuals of the North undertook much other work for the Negro but little of it had any economic bearing. The work of extremists in churches and in schools had bad results in irritating the races, while the natural effect of the gift in 1867 of political privilege was unsettling from an economic standpoint. The Negro received much advice and assistance to help him get his political and social rights, but little attention was paid to his material condition.

ECONOMIC ENVIRONMENT OF THE EMANCIPATED NEGRO

The influences surrounding the emancipated Negro were contradictory; some tended to elevate him, others to lower him. Until the strict drawing of race lines by the prejudices arising out of Reconstruction there was a noticeable tendency among the emancipated to separate into economic and social classes. Between the more intelligent mulattoes and the blacks there was a slight antipathy. Most of those who were free before the war were mulattoes and many of them had property; in Louisiana they formed an important part of the colored population, holding property valued in 1860 at $13,000,000. The house servants held themselves superior to the field workers. The natural aristocrats of the colored people, with the better training and the superior intelligence, might have been expected under favorable conditions to become the economic leaders.

There was a universal desire to own land, to

obtain an education, and to be like the old masters. There was enthusiasm to get all the good that freedom could give, but conflicting with this was a general notion that freedom meant either less work or no work. Negro women frequently declined to work in the fields or as servants. Negro men proved that they were free by neglecting their crops to go hunting and fishing and to camp meeting. Intemperance was widespread, while swindlers found the credulous people an easy prey, and the savings went for such luxuries as excursions, circuses, jewelry, and subscription books. After a while too many of the abler Negroes went into politics instead of farming. Though land was cheap the Negroes secured titles to but little of it. Most of them became tenants, and after a period of experimentation the share system was adopted to govern the division between landlord and tenant. This, with the accompanying credit system and crop-lien was good enough at such a time to enable a very thrifty and energetic laborer to get a start, but for the average Negro it meant the removal of incentive to progress. Those who purchased land were frequently tricked by rascals into buying bad titles.

The result was that the better class of Negroes in a few years went to the towns and cities; the whites of the black belt gradually left the plantations for the villages and cities and entered the industries or the professions. So with absentee landlords and inefficient overseers the Negro tenants were left more and more to their own incompetent ways. The removal of the personal control of the whites from the Black Belt caused the industrious Negroes to suffer from the thieving of the worthless ones. No longer could poultry, pigs, sheep, and other domestic animals be raised. Excessive hospitality—in part a result of the solid race feeling—made it difficult for an industrious Negro to save anything, for his trifling friends and relatives would descend upon him and consume his substance. The crop stealing evil, which was not checked until after Reconstruction, also helped to keep down the honest and industrious Negro. The former wealthy sections, such as the interior Black Belt and the Sea Island cotton and rice country, were not for years again developed for agriculture. In general the outlook for the economic independence of the race was not favorable. Under such conditions the most sensible assistance that could have been given was the opportunity for self-help and training in thrift and economy by the Freedmen's Bank.

REFERENCES

This account of economic conditions among the Negroes is based upon the following authorities:

Andrews, *The South since the War.*

Avary, *Dixie after the War.*

Botume, *First Days among the Contrabands.*

Dixon, W. H., *White Conquest.*

Eaton, *Grant, Lincoln and the Freedmen.*

Fleming, W. L., *Civil War and Reconstruction in Alabama.*

Fleming, W. L., *Documentary History of Reconstruction,* Vol I, pp. 9-95; Vol. II, pp. 276, 298.

Freedmen's Bureau Reports, 1865-1869.

Garner, J. W., *Reconstruction in Mississippi.*

Knox, *Whip, Hoe and Sword.*

Latham, *White and Black.*
Leigh, Frances B., *Ten Years on a Georgia Plantation since the War.*
Pearson, *Letters from Port Royal.*
Peirce, *Freedmen's Bureau.*
Reid, *After the War.*
Reports of the various Freedmen's Aid Societies, 1862–1866.
Towne, Laura M., *Letters* and *Diary*, Edited by Holland.
Trowbridge, *The South.*

Chapter II

ORIGIN OF THE FREEDMEN'S
SAVINGS BANK

THE ALLOTMENT SYSTEM AND THE
MILITARY BANKS

BEFORE the close of the Civil War several experiments had been tried with savings banks for Negroes. Nearly all of these were established at large army posts for the purpose of preventing the soldiers from squandering their pay and bounty money—almost the first money they had ever handled.

When the United States government began to pay the Negro soldiers as white soldiers were paid, it was found that few made good use of the money received. The regimental sutlers as well as swindlers of every kind were always ready for pay day in a Negro regiment, and had little difficulty in getting most of the soldiers' cash. In Massachusetts the friends of the Negro, anxious for the black troops to save something, induced the state authorities to establish in Negro regiments accredited to that state the savings or "allotment" system then in operation among the white troops. Under this plan the regimental paymasters were authorized to permit the soldiers to "allot" a certain part of their pay each month to a relative for the use of the latter, or

19

allot it to the government for savings which would be paid to the soldiers when discharged. Since most Negro soldiers were unable to reach their families, the "allotment" system enabled some willing ones to save part of their pay until they were mustered out and in need of the funds.[1]

The first bank established for Negroes only was organized in New Orleans in 1864 by General N. P. Banks, who called it the "Free Labor Bank." There were several thousand Negro soldiers in Bank's command and many "free men of color" with property in New Orleans, and on the plantations in the parishes under Federal control there were other thousands of half-free Negroes who received or were promised some sort of pay for their work. General Banks was much interested in his "free labor department," which was designed for the purpose of transforming the late slaves into free working men. It was mainly for these "free laborers" that the bank was established, though soldiers were also encouraged to make deposits. The bank was a success, according to report, though full information concerning it is lacking. Not only were individual deposits received but the officers in charge of the Negro "home colonies" placed in the bank the proceeds from the plantation sales. For example, the deposits of the Rost Home Colony amounted to $21,605.83.[2]

[1] *Senate Rept.*, No. 440, 46 Cong., 2 Sess. (1880); *Booklet, Freedmen's Savings and Trust Co.* (1872).

[2] This colony was established on the Destrehan plantation of Judge Pierre A. Rost. Probably the money came to the bank through the Freedmen's Bureau.—*House Exec. Doc.*, No. 144, 44 Cong., 1 Sess.; Phelps, *Louisiana*, p. 330; Howard's *Reminiscences*; Peirce, *Freedmen's Bureau*, pp. 18, 123; Banks, "Emancipated Labor in Louisiana," *New York Times*,

In the same year military savings banks, intended primarily for the use of Negro soldiers, were established by General B. F. Butler at Norfolk, Virginia, and by General Rufus Saxton at Beaufort, South Carolina. At these places there were not only regiments of Negro troops, but there were also large numbers of other Negroes who, as a result of Federal military occupation, had been free from their owners since 1861 or soon after, and who, for several years, had been learning how to work for themselves.[3] But the Negro soldiers were the best depositors. They were now paid regularly each month and many of them had received large bounties upon enlisting; they were fed and clothed by the government and needed to spend but little of their pay. Accordingly they welcomed the establishment of the banks, and many of them made deposits which remained until the close of the war. The total of deposits is not known, but when the war ended the Beaufort Bank had on hand about $200,000, a large part of which consisted of unclaimed deposits of soldiers who had disappeared. Some of them had been mustered out of service or transferred to other posts; others had been killed in action or had died of disease, and their relatives could not be found; and many of those who had placed money in the bank were too ignorant to draw

February 11, 1864. Judge Rost of Louisiana was a diplomatic representative of the Confederacy in Europe, 1862–1865. His Destrehan plantation in St. Charles parish was confiscated when the Union forces came in, and on it was established a Negro refugee or "home" colony.

[3] See Pearson, *Letters from Port Royal*, and Holland *Letters and Diary of Laura M. Towne*.

it out. Consequently at the close of the Civil War these large unclaimed sums prevented the military banks from winding up their business.[4]

PLANS OF SPERRY AND ALVORD

When the war was drawing to a close it was evident that something must be done to safeguard the unclaimed deposits in the military banks, and since large sums in pay and bounty were still due the Negro soldiers, it was also believed that a plan ought to be devised to help them save something. So, early in 1865, two distinct efforts were being made to organize permanent savings banks for the benefit of the Negroes. The first attempt was made by A. M. Sperry, an army paymaster, and several associates. They planned to found an institution which they hoped would be endorsed by the United States government, and would then absorb and continue the military savings banks at Norfolk and Beaufort and the Free Labor Bank in New Orleans, and with its branches would also serve as a savings bank for the Negro soldiers still in service. The Negro troops were being mustered out more slowly than the white troops, and it was expected that several thousand would be retained in the regular service. Moreover, there were thousands of Negro soldiers who had unsettled claims against the United States for pay and bounty. Sperry expected to have an agent of the bank with each Negro regiment for the purpose of soliciting deposits and arranging for

[4] Douglas Report in *House Rept.*, No. 502, 44 Cong., 1 Sess. (1876), 24; Bruce Report in *Senate Rept.*, No. 440, 46 Cong., 2 Sess, 24; Douglass, *Life and Times*, p. 487.

the collection of claims against the government. It is uncertain whether or not he intended to solicit deposits from Negroes who were not in the Army.[5]

The other banking scheme was promoted by John W. Alvord who finally succeeded in uniting Sperry's efforts with his own and in securing the incorporation by Congress of the Freedmen's Savings and Trust Company. Alvord was a Congregational minister who, for a time, was an attaché of Sherman's army, probably a chaplain. In Savannah during the winter of 1864–1865 he had observed the condition of the blacks and had seen the inauguration of Sherman's colonization scheme on the confiscated lands of the Georgia and South Carolina coasts.[6]

In later years the investigating committees of Congress treated Alvord and his associates without mercy, but there is reason to believe that they were too severe on Alvord at least.[7]

[5] Bruce Rept., p. 246; *Sen. Misc. Doc.*, No. 88, 43 Cong., 2 Sess.

[6] See Sherman's S. O. No. 15, in Fleming, *Documentary History of Reconstruction*, I, 350.

[7] The following quotation is from the report of the Douglas Committee: "The chief and founder of the so-called Freedmen's Bank was one John W. Alvord, an attaché of the Bureau and superintendent of its educational department. This man, who had been anything but a success, abounding in platitudes about the good of mankind in general, but with a keen eye to the main chance at the same time, having failed in both lay and clerical pursuits in other sections, now turned his benevolent regards to the confiding and ignorant black element of the South. He got up the charter for the bank, a charter so singular in its array of high and eminent names for incorporators, for its business organization whereby nine out of fifty trustees were constituted a quorum, and so utterly and entirely without safeguards or protection for those who were to become its patrons and depositors that it is hard to believe that its author, whatever might have been his other deficiencies, did not thoroughly understand how to organize cunning against simplicity and make it pay for being cheated." *Ho. Rept.*, No. 502, 44 Cong. 1 Sess.

While connected with the Freedmen's Bank, Alvord was also general superintendent of education for the Freedmen's Bureau, an institution which attracted a great deal of unfavorable criticism.[8]

After his return to the North from Savannah, Alvord and his associates worked out a plan for a Negro savings bank which should be conducted under the patronage of the United States government, and on January 27, 1865, he secured a meeting of interested business men and philanthropists at the National Exchange Bank in New York City. To them he explained the proposed bank and convinced them of the necessity for it and of its practicability. Those present at the meeting were: Peter Cooper, W. C. Bryant, Hiram Barney, Charles Collins, Thomas Denny, Walter S. Griffith, William Allen, Abraham Baldwin, R. S. Barnes, S. B. Caldwell, R. R. Graves, A. S. Hatch, Walter S. Hatch, E. A. Lambert, Roe Lockwood, R. H. Manning, R. W. Ropes, A. H. Wallis, George Whipple and Albert Woodruff. They adopted plans for the organization of the bank and for its incorporation by Congress.[9] The action of these prominent men would, it seems, endorse the respectability, if not the business capacity, of Alvord.

INCORPORATION OF THE FREEDMEN'S SAVINGS BANK

The next step was to secure a charter from

[8] See Peirce, *Freedmen's Bureau.*

[9] Bruce Rept., p. 246; Rept. of J. J. Knox, Comptroller of the Currency, Feb. 21, 1873, in *Sen. Misc. Doc.*, No. 88, 43 Cong. 2 Sess.

Congress. A bill to incorporate the Freedmen's Savings and Trust Company was introduced into the Senate by Henry W. Wilson of Massachusetts, on February 13, 1865. It was referred to the Committee on Slavery and Freedmen, of which Charles Sumner was chairman. On February 18, Senator Sumner reported the bill with slight changes and on March 2 moved its consideration. In answer to an objection Sumner stated that it conferred no extraordinary privileges, that it was an ordinary savings bank charter, and that its "object is a simple charity." Senator Buckalew, of Pennsylvania, a member of the committee that considered and reported the bill, said that the only question was "whether we ought to establish such an institution outside of the District of Columbia." Senator Powell, of Kentucky, objected that the bill gave "a roving kind of commission for these persons to establish a savings bank in any part of the United States." "I think," he said, "the bill is wholly unconstitutional. I do not believe that Congress has any right to establish a savings bank outside of the District of Columbia."

An amendment was then adopted which limited the location of the bank to the District of Columbia, and the bill was passed by the Senate. The next day, March 3, one day before the end of the session, Representative Eliot of Massachusetts introduced into the House a bill which was supposed to be the one which had been passed by the Senate, but upon examination it was found that the amendment limiting the location of the bank to the District of Columbia had not been inserted. The House then added an amendment slightly different from the Senate amendment, though believed by Eliot to be identical. Objection was made that the District of Columbia was not represented on the board of trustees named in the bill, and Eliot met this objection by inserting the name of Chief Justice Salmon P. Chase. Thus amended the bill passed the House.[10]

Since the bills as passed by the Senate and the House were not exactly alike, the action of a conference committee would, under ordinary circumstances, be necessary in order to harmonize them; but it seems that no one noticed the slight differences. The record states that the bill was signed by President Lincoln on the same day, March 3. It is said that when Lincoln signed it he remarked: "This bank is just what the freedmen need." He signed at the same time the act creating the Freedmen's Bureau.[11]

The bill which was presented to President Lincoln for his approval was neither the bill passed by the Senate nor the one passed by the House but was the original bill introduced into the Senate by Senator Wilson with the words "in the City of Washington, in the District of Columbia" inserted by some one in the body of the bill. The name of Salmon P. Chase as a member of the Board of Trustees was omitted. This was the bill that was published as law. In

[10] *Cong. Globe*, 38 Cong., 2 Sess., pt. I, p. 776, and pt. II, pp. 885, 1311; *Senate Misc. Doc.*, No. 88, 43 Cong., 2 Sess.

[11] *Cong. Globe*, 38 Cong., 2 Sess., pt. II, p. 1403; *Booklet, Freedmen's Savings and Trust Company*, 1872; Fleming, *Documentary History of Reconstruction*, I, 319.

the hurry and confusion incident upon the close of the session, this substitution of the bills was not noticed; it has never been explained; it may have been a mistake due to carelessness, or it may have been intentional. Some years later there was a disposition on the part of critics to search for ulterior motives behind these changes. But the only important difference was the omission of the name of Chief Justice Chase.[12]

[12] In most of the unofficial copies of the law published at the time the amendment fixing the location of the bank at Washington, District of Columbia, is omitted. The *Nation* and *The Banker's Magazine* both asserted ten years later that the District of Columbia amendment and the Chase amendment also were purposely omitted from the enrolled bill. But in the laws published in the *Globe*, 38 Cong., 2 Sess., appendix, p. 143, only the name of Chase is omitted. *Cong. Globe*, 38 Cong., 2 Sess., pt. II, pp. 1371, 1391, 1403; *Banker's Magazine*, June 1875; *The Nation*, April 15, 1875.

Chapter III

ORGANIZATION AND EXPANSION OF THE FREEDMEN'S BANK

THE ACT OF INCORPORATION

FIFTY men, most of them well known, were named in the Freedmen's Bank Act of March 3, 1865, as incorporators and trustees.[1] These were: Peter Cooper, William C. Bryant, A. A. Low, S. B. Chittenden, Charles H. Marshall, William A. Booth, Gerritt Smith, William A. Hall, William Allen, John Jay, Abraham Baldwin, A. S. Barnes, Hiram Barney, Seth B. Hunt, Samuel Holmes, Charles Collins, R. R. Graves, Walter S. Griffith, A. H. Wallis, D. S. Gregory, J. W. Alvord, George Whipple, A. S. Hatch, E. A. Lambert, W. G. Lambert, Roe Lockwood, R. H. Manning, R. W. Ropes, Walter T. Hatch, Albert Woodruff, and Thomas Denney, of New York; John M. Forbes, William Claflin, S. G. Howe, George L. Stearnes, Edward Atkinson, A. A. Lawrence, and John M. S. Williams, of Massachusetts; Edward Harris and Thomas Davis of Rhode Island; Stephen Colwell, J. Wheaton Smith, Francis E. Cope, Thomas Webster, B. S. Hunt, and Henry Samuel, of Pennsylvania; Edward Harwood, Adam Poe, Levi Coffin, and J. M. Walden, of Ohio. The trustees were

[1] See appendix, p. 131.

29

given the power to fill vacancies in their ranks, at least ten votes being necessary for the election of a trustee. Meetings of the board were to be held once a month or oftener, and if a trustee neglected for six months to attend the meetings his successor might be appointed. The trustees were to elect from their number a president and two vice-presidents. Nine trustees, of whom one must be the president or a vice-president, constituted a quorum, and at least seven affirmative votes were required to authorize any investment, sale, or transfer of securities. The list of trustees contained the names of many prominent men, but the Douglas Report (1876) on the affairs of the bank asserted that some of them did not consent to the use of their names and did not accept or exercise office.[2]

The business of the institution was to be confined to the Negro race. The object of the corporation, as stated in the act, was to receive deposits offered "by or in behalf of persons heretofore held in slavery in the United States, or their descendants." At least two-thirds of the deposits must be invested in securities of the United States, one-third being held on deposit or otherwise as an "available fund" for current needs.

[2] "Many of the distinguished and eminently worthy gentlemen who figure in the Charter never gave the use of their names and never accepted or undertook to execute the trust it created. They were thrust in for appearance's sake and to make the delusion attractive and complete. Some who really believed in the good professions of the projectors of the scheme and its adaptability to promote the welfare of those for whose benefit it was apparently intended, and who at first took seats at the board of trustees, quickly vacated them in disgust and the whole management devolved, as was manifestly the intention that it should do, upon a cabal in Washington consisting of a small minority of the acting trustees."—*Ho. Rept.* No. 502, 44 Cong., 1 Sess.

Not more than seven per cent was to be allowed as interest on deposits, and should any interest remain uncalled for two years after the death of a depositor it might be applied to the education of Negro children, and the principal was also to be so applied if not claimed within seven years. Persons connected with the institution directly or indirectly as trustees, officials, or employees were not to be allowed to borrow from it. None of the trustees was to receive any compensation except the president and the vice-presidents, who were supposed to give active service, and all salaries and the bonds of the officials were to be fixed by the trustees. The books of the bank were at all times to be open to the inspection of the agents of Congress.[3]

Such were the principal provisions of the Freedmen's Bank charter. The law would seem to confine the business of the bank to the District of Columbia, and Congress certainly so intended, as was shown by the discussions in the House and in the Senate. On the other hand the documents show that from the beginning the incorporators meant to establish headquarters in New York City with branch banks in each southern state. There were in the act no penal clauses to bind the officials, and nothing definite was provided in regard to their bonds. The trustees were not made liable personally, probably because of the quasi-charitable nature of their services, and because of the high character and prominence of some of the individuals involved. It was not then

[3] *Acts and Resolutions*, 38 Cong., 2 Sess., p. 99; Fleming, *Documentary History of Reconstruction*, I, 382; *Ho. Misc. Doc.* No. 16, 43 Cong., 2 Sess., p. 85.

known that most of the directors were to be
"dummies." Besides, the law was specific as to
the disposition to be made of the deposits—two
thirds must be invested in United States securities and the remainder must be held in "available" form. As Congress might have the books
inspected at will, no misuse of the funds seemed
possible.

ORGANIZATION OF THE BANK

The trustees elected as president William A.
Booth[4] of New York, and, as had been planned,
established headquarters in New York City.
Alvord, who was now inspector and superintendent of schools for the Freedmen's Bureau, was
made corresponding secretary of the bank. The
salary of President Booth was fixed at $1,000, it
being understood that his duties would be merely
nominal.[5] Alvord's duties were to travel through
the southern states organizing branch banks and
soliciting deposits. His position as inspector of
the Freedmen's Bureau schools under General
Howard would enable him all the more success-
fully to perform his work as bank missionary.
Paymaster Sperry, who with his associates had
been endeavoring to consolidate and perpetuate
the military savings banks, had recognized the
advantages of Alvord's scheme and had joined

[4] Wm. A. Booth (1805–1895) was a prominent banker of New York
City. The only available sketch of his life makes no mention of his connection with the Freedmen's Bank. (*National Cyclopedia of Biography*,
10: 382.)

[5] *Booklet, Freedmen's Savings Bank*, 1867. In 1867 the officers were
Mahlon H. Hewitt, president; John W. Alvord, first vice-president;
Lewis Clephane, second vice-president; D. L. Eaton, actuary. In 1868
Alvord became president. The presidents before him seem to have had
little to do with the administration of the institution.

forces with him before the act of incorporation was passed. Sperry's experience as paymaster to Negro troops made him a valuable man and he now became a soliciting agent for the Freedmen's Savings Bank.[6]

BEGINNING OF EXPANSION

Although there was nothing in the charter that would authorize the establishment of branch banks or headquarters outside the District of Columbia, Alvord's original plan had contemplated extension by branches into all Negro districts. The incorporators who were directing the policy of the bank, perhaps through ignorance, paid no attention to the will of Congress as expressed in the debates over the act of incorporation and in the amendments, but proceeded to expand the system.[7]

Organization and expansion proceeded rapidly. The New York headquarters office was established on April 4, 1865. On May 16 the New York branch bank received the first deposits, and on June 8 its deposits amounted to $700.00.[8] On June 3 Butler's military savings bank at Norfolk, Virginia, was absorbed with its unclaimed deposits of soldiers amounting to $7,956.38. The military savings bank established by General Saxton at Beaufort, South Carolina, became a branch of the Freedmen's Bank on December 14,

[6] Douglas Report, pp. 30, 66; Bruce Report, p. 246.

[7] The Comptroller of the Currency in a report dated February 21, 1873, takes the position that under the charter there was no authority for the branches.—*Sen. Misc. Doc.* No. 88, 43 Cong., 2 Sess.

[8] *Booklet, Freedmen's Savings Bank,* 1872, containing the first report to the trustees.

1865, and from it the New York branch secured
$170,000 of soldiers' unclaimed deposits. The
New Orleans "Free Labor Bank" was not taken
in until January, 1866. The total deposits in this
bank are not given in the records, but one fund
was included which amounted to more than
$20,000, presumably representing profits from
the Rost Home Colony.[9] On July 11, 1865,[10] a
branch bank was established in Washington,
District of Columbia, and a month later its deposits amounted to $843.84.[11]

Effective work was done by Alvord and
Sperry, who went south in the fall of 1865 to
organize branches in each southern state and
to secure deposits. Sperry obtained permission
from the War Department to accompany the
Negro troops and to be present at the army pay
tables in order to solicit deposits from the soldiers. He went with the army to the Mexican
border and secured deposits amounting to
$120,000 from the Negro regiments of the
25th Army Corps. Soon after his return Sperry
became an inspector of branch banks.

[9] See chapter 1. The affairs of the Rost Home Colony were never
straightened out. It is impossible to say anything with certainty as to
what finally became of the money belonging to this colony. The plantation belonging to Judge Rost was worked by Negroes under the supervision of the Freedmen's Bureau. According to some accounts $15,000
or more was cleared in 1866 and by order of General Howard this amount
was placed in the New Orleans branch to be used for Negro education.
Under the Freedmen's Bureau Act of 1866 this money should have been
deposited in the United States Treasury. But later it was invested in
5:20's and transferred from New Orleans to the Freedmen's Bank in
Washington, D. C. Finally, by some trick of bookkeeping it was withdrawn into private hands and disappeared. Douglas Report, pp. 182–187.
See below, p. 97.

[10] August 1 is another date given.

[11] *Ho. Misc. Doc.* No. 16, 43 Cong., 2 Sess., p. 91; *Sen. Misc. Doc.*
No. 88, 43 Cong., 2 Sess., pp. 2, 3; Bruce Report, p. 246; Douglas
Report, p. 66.

THE FREEDMEN'S BANK AND THE
FREEDMEN'S BUREAU

In many ways the Freedmen's Bank was connected with the Freedmen's Bureau, and the connection was used to every possible advantage. The Negroes came to believe that the bank was a part of the Freedmen's Bureau system. When he went south in the interest of the bank, Alvord found that his connection with the Freedmen's Bureau educational department was of decided advantage to him in his work. He carried with him the endorsement of General O. O. Howard, the Commissioner of the Bureau,[12] and he is said to have represented this recommendation as an order from Howard that the Negro soldiers should deposit their bounty money with him. "It appears also," asserted later investigators, "that Howard directed that bounty money in the hands of Bureau officials be turned over to the Bank."[13]

For five years Alvord, as inspector of the Bureau schools and as officer of the bank, traversed the South soliciting deposits and establishing branch banks. He continued this work for two years after he became president, for in this field he was considered most valuable by those who were directing the policy of the institution. To meetings of Negroes he explained its purposes and told of its advantages. He, Sperry, and other agents scattered circulars broadcast explaining the benefits of the bank, and stating that Lincoln had favored it, and that General Howard con-

[12] Howard's Statement. See Appendix, p. 146.
[13] Douglas Report, p. 67.

sidered it essential to the welfare of the ex-slaves. The Negroes were given to understand that the institution was absolutely safe, since it was under the guarantee of Congress and had its funds invested in United States securities which were good as long as the government should last. The fact was also emphasized that it was a benevolent scheme solely for the benefit of those who had once been slaves. The profits, they were told, would be returned to the depositors as interest, or would be expended for Negro education.

The Douglas Report (1876) criticized severely the methods of the promoters, charging, among other things: "In regard to this bank the grossest deception was practiced upon the Negroes. They were told that it was a government institution and its solvency and safety guaranteed by the United States. Missionaries, of whom the chief was Alvord, perambulated the South, mixing religion, politics and education, and teaching the blacks how to 'toil and save' and then trust their hard earned savings to Alvord and his associates to invest them, not until, however, they had levied toll for their services in bestowing such inestimable benefits and for their disinterested labors and sacrifices."[14]

The Freedmen's Bureau was soon more closely associated with the bank. George W. Balloch, then chief disbursing officer of the Bureau, later a trustee of the bank, gave material aid by allowing the offices of the Bureau agents throughout the South to be used rent-free by the branch banks; and often the agents acted without charge

[14] *Ho. Report* No. 502, 44 Cong., 1 Sess.

as cashiers. So it came about that for a time nearly every bank official wore the uniform of the United States; the Bureau offices and the branch banks were often in the same rooms; and the missionaries and agents of the Bureau regularly solicited deposits. The effect of its connection with the Bureau was to make the depositors believe that they were dealing with the United States government, and there is no doubt that in order to increase the business and extend the system this belief was intentionally fostered.[15]

There are in the records numerous references to the close relationship existing between bank and Bureau. Alvord, for example, in a report to General Howard in 1866 concerning Bureau schools, mentions: "The Savings and Trust Company for Freedmen, chartered by Congress last winter and *placed under your advisement.*"[16] Later, before the investigating committees, depositors frequently stated that they were made to understand that the institution was conducted by the United States. Sanders Howell made this statement to the Douglas Committee: "Mr. Wilson, who was cashier of the bank,[17] stated

[15] Bruce Report, pp. 180, 246, and Appendix, p. 45; Douglas Report, pp. 66, 67; *Ho. Misc. Doc.* No. 18, 49 Cong., 1 Sess., and No. 34, 49 Cong., 2 Sess.; *Sen. Misc. Doc.* No. 10, 47 Cong., 2 Sess.; Report of Alvord, Jan. 1, 1866, in *Ho. Ex. Doc.* No. 70, 39 Cong., 1 Sess.; Bradford's speech in *Cong. Record*, April 22, 1876; Howard Investigation, pp. 51, 53, in *Ho. Report.* No. 121, 41 Cong., 2 Sess.; *Banker's Magazine*, June, 1875; *The Nation*, April 15, 1875; Douglass, *Life and Times*, p. 487; Somers, *Southern States since the War*, p. 54; Peirce, *Freedmen's Bureau, passim; Senate Misc. Doc.* No. 88, 43 Cong., 2 Sess.; Committee on Banking and Currency, Hearings on Freedmen's Savings and Trust Company, 1910.

[16] *Ho. Ex. Doc.* No. 70, 39 Cong., 1 Sess.

[17] The branch bank in Washington.

that the government was bound for every dollar and that the money was placed in government bonds, otherwise I should not have put my money in there."[18]

THE BRANCH BANKS

Success attended the efforts of the bank promoters. Before the end of 1865 ten branches had been organized, and during 1866 ten more were established. In all, there were established thirty-four branches, thirty-two of which were in the southern states.[19]

LIST OF BRANCH BANKS WITH DATES OF ESTABLISHMENT

1865
Beaufort, S. C.
Huntsville, Ala.
Memphis, Tenn.
Louisville, Ky.
Nashville, Tenn.
Norfolk, Va.
Richmond, Va.
Wilmington, N. C.
Washington, D. C.
Vicksburg, Miss.

1866
Augusta, Ga.
Baltimore, Md.
Charleston, S. C.
Jacksonville, Fla.
Tallahassee, Fla.

Mobile, Ala.
New York City.
Savannah, Ga.
New Bern, N. C.
New Orleans, La.

1867
None organized.

1868
St. Louis, Mo.
Raleigh, N. C.
Macon, Ga.

1869
Chattanooga, Tenn.

[18] Douglas Report, p. 117; Peirce, *Freedmen's Bureau*, p. 153.

[19] *Seventh Annual Report of Freedmen's Savings and Trust Company; Ho. Misc. Doc.* No. 16, 43 Cong., 2 Sess., p. 85.

1870	Philadelphia, Pa.
Atlanta, Ga.	Shreveport, La.
Columbus, Miss.	
Lexington, Ky.	*1871-72*
Little Rock, Ark.	Columbia, Tenn.
Montgomery, Ala.	Lynchburg, Va.
Natchez, Miss.	

The disturbing force of Reconstruction politics is seen in the sudden checking of expansion in 1867 and the slow increase afterward. Headquarters remained in New York until March, 1868, when the principal office was moved to Washington and Alvord was elected president.[20] A good building was erected in Washington[21] opposite the United States Treasury, at a cost of $260,000. This expenditure for a building was probably contrary to law, as was also the investment at this time by the branch banks of $160,000 in real estate.

INTERLOCKING BOARDS

The trustees of the bank were frequently members of other boards which had business relations with the bank. Among the prominent Freedmen's Bureau officials who were connected with the Freedmen's Bank as trustees were General O. O. Howard, General C. H. Howard, General G. W. Balloch, General E. Whittlesey, D. L. Eaton, and J. W. Alvord. These men, except Alvord and Eaton, were also army officers, and

[20] The officers in 1869 were: John W. Alvord, president; Louis Clephane, first vice-president; Rev. D. W. Anderson, second vice-president; D. L. Eaton, actuary; S. L. Harris, general inspector; R. B. Hunt, assistant inspector.—*Booklet, Freedmen's Savings Bank*, 1869.

[21] On Pennsylvania Avenue and Lafayette Square.

each was a member of from three to eight other boards or organizations more or less closely related to one another in the capacity of borrower and lender or of purchaser and seller. Many minor officials were likewise connected with similarly related enterprises. It was this identity of personnel which gave some foundation for the charges against the so-called "Freedmen's Bureau ring" which for a time controlled the Bureau, the bank, the freedmen's schools, Howard University, several commercial enterprises and religious organizations, and a few political undertakings.[22]

Somewhat later, about 1870, the Bureau's influence began to wane, as a new element began to contest its control. These newcomers were from the District of Columbia and were connected with such interests as the First National Bank, the District of Columbia government, the Seneca Sandstone Company, the Metropolitan Paving Company, the American Building Block Company, and other such organizations.[23] This state of affairs was sure, sooner or later, to affect the bank unfavorably.

[22] See, e.g., Fernando Wood's charges, Peirce, *Freedmen's Bureau*, pp. 110, 111, 117, 153.

[23] See below, chapter 5.

Chapter IV

THE GOOD WORK OF THE BANK

METHODS OF ADMINISTRATION

THE organization and plan of operation of the bank appeared in the beginning to be practicable and effective. As an Alabama Democratic Congressman said, "It was the very contrivance that was needed by these people [the Negroes] above all others."[1] From the principal office in New York, later in Washington, the business of the entire system was controlled, and to it daily, weekly, and monthly reports were sent up from the branches. All deposits made at the branches, with the exception of small amounts for current expenses, were sent to the central office to be invested in United States bonds.

The cashiers and other officials were supposed to be men of high character, chosen because of their interest in the welfare of the freedmen. Most of them were, at first, officials of the Freedmen's Bureau or of the Army, and several of them were ministers—missionaries sent south to work among the lately emancipated. Few Negroes were at first found among the officials or employees. They were not yet competent. Some of the prominent trustees, such as Ketchum of

[1] Speech of Bradford of Alabama in *Cong. Record*, April 22, 1876, p. 2701.

New York, took a genuine interest in the bank, attended the board meetings, helped with affairs, and gave advice to the inexperienced administrative force.[2]

Before the charter was amended in 1870, no loans could be made by the principal bank or by the branches, for, by the law of 1865, two thirds of all deposits must be invested in United States securities and the remainder held as an available fund. After 1870, when Congress permitted the bank to make loans on real estate, the branch banks in a few cities were permitted large privileges; but, as a rule, to the last, the branch banks simply gathered in the money and sent to Washington all that they did not pay back to depositors as interest or as withdrawals.

An inspector traveled constantly among the branches, examining the books and endeavoring to keep the accounts in good order. The first inspector was ex-Paymaster A. M. Sperry, who had assisted in organizing some of the branches and who had secured large sums for deposit from the Negro soldiers. Sperry, who was a good man for this post, did much to keep the business in order, but he was heavily overworked. After a time he was given an assistant inspector.

TRAINING OF NEGRO BUSINESS MEN

In the branch banks, and at Washington after 1868 when the headquarters were removed to that city, a body of Negro business men was being trained. There was a growing sentiment that, since the bank was for the benefit of the

[2] Bruce Report, p. 178.

Negroes, it should have as many Negro officials as possible, and in time about one half of the employees were Negroes. At nearly all of the branches, especially after 1870, when some of them were allowed to do a regular banking business,[3] there was an advisory council, or board of directors, of responsible Negro property holders. These men were proud of the Freedmen's Bank and of their connection with it.

For example, National Bank Inspector Meigs gave special praise to the Negro board of advisers of the Norfolk branch who, he said, "are very proud of the position they occupy." And of the Richmond branch he said: "They have what is called an advisory board of colored men of the better class and these men evidently take a deep interest in the welfare of the institution and promote in every way the habit of saving on the part of their people."[4]

LITERATURE OF THE BANK

The more thrifty Negroes, believing that their deposits would be secure in these banks, which they understood were supported by the government, eagerly availed themselves of the opportunity to lay up small sums for the future. To each depositor a unique pass book was given. In this book were the usual printed rules governing the making and withdrawal of deposits, a list of the branches of the bank, with names of the cashiers, and this statement:

[3] These were at Norfolk, Va., Beaufort, S. C., and Jacksonville, Fla.

[4] There were whites on some of the local boards. Report of Meigs, National Bank Inspector, in *Ho. Misc. Doc.* No. 16, 43 Cong., 2 Sess., p. 64; Bruce Report, pp. 246, 247.

This is a benevolent institution. All profits go to the depositors, or to educational purposes for the freedmen and their descendants.

The whole institution is under the charter of Congress, and received the commendation and counsel of the President, Abraham Lincoln. One of the last official acts of his valued life was the signing of the bill which gave existence to this bank.

On the cover, also, was the following commendation from General Howard, which was to the Negro sufficient proof of its connection with the Bureau:

I consider the Freedmen's Savings and Trust Company to be greatly needed by the colored people, and have welcomed it as an auxiliary to the Freedmen's Bureau.
—*Major-General O. O. Howard.*

For the purpose of educating the depositor in thrift a table was printed in the book to show the possibilities of a small saving each day:

A man who saves ten cents a day for ten years, will have, if he puts it at interest at six per cent:

In 1 year	$ 36.99
In 2 years	76.20
In 3 years	117.81
In 4 years	161.94
In 5 years	208.74
In 6 years	258.42
In 7 years	311.13
In 8 years	367.03
In 9 years	426.37
In 10 years	489.31

There were, in one edition of the book, pictures of Lincoln, Grant, Howard, and the United States flag, and some verses, which, as charged by unfriendly critics, the Negroes believed were written by General Howard:

'Tis little by little the bee fills her cell;
And little by little a man sinks a well;
'Tis little by little a bird builds her nest;
By littles a forest in verdure is drest.
'Tis little by little great volumes are made;
By littles a mountain or levels are made;
'Tis little by little an ocean is filled;
And little by little a city we build.
'Tis little by little an ant gets her store;
Every little we add to a little makes more;
Step by step we walk miles, and we sew stitch by stitch;
Word by word we read books, cent by cent we grow rich.[5]

On the pass book used in New York City was printed in English, French, and German this legend: "The Government of the United States has made this bank perfectly safe."[6]

Pamphlet material concerning the bank was issued in large quantities and circulated among the Negroes. There were reports in popular form giving information about the number and location of the branches, the number of depositors and the amounts of deposits, and the rules regulating the business. And once or twice a year booklets were published for distribution which contained good advice in regard to thrift, assertions that the bank had the approval of President Lincoln, and that it was "based solely on the faith and credit of the United States," tables of gains, poems on thrift, suggestions to teachers on how to teach children to save and on how to save money by abstaining from whiskey and

[5] The later editions of the pass book omitted most of this material. With similar matter it was then printed in the pamphlets which were distributed.

[6] Committee on Banking and Currency, Hearings 1910; *Ho. Misc. Doc.* No. 16, 43 Cong., 2 Sess., pp. 83, 85 and No. 34, 49 Cong., 2 Sess.; Douglas Report, p. 22, *et passim.*

tobacco, and maxims of economy such as, "Save your dimes and buy you a home or a farm."[7]

GOOD RESULTS

As a factor in Negro education there was then probably nothing better than this literature and the bank it represented and the good effects were soon observed. Many Negroes, who a few months before had been slaves, began to save and make deposits. It became the fashion to have a bank account, no matter how small. Sums were received from five cents up, and on deposits of $1.00 or more interest was paid semi-annually at the rate of six per cent. Of course the deposits of a year were not much larger than the withdrawals, but according to bank officials the money drawn out was often spent intelligently. The Negro would put money into the bank during the summer and fall to be used in the winter and spring when supplies were scarce. Thrift was encouraged; many saved in order to purchase homes, or to purchase farm stock and implements. Less money was spent for whiskey and for articles of worthless finery so dear to the African heart. The Negroes who had bank books were less easily swindled by the multitude of sharpers who came to teach them the ways of freemen. Many years later Booker T. Washington declared: "No work was ever undertaken for the benefit of the Freedmen more laudable in its purpose or more designed to assist a people who had just come out of slavery to get on their feet."[8]

[7] Booklets, etc. *Freedmen's Savings Bank*, 1867–1872. See Appendix. pp. 144–146.

[8] Washington, *Story of the Negro*, II, p. 214. See also Brawley, *Short History of the American Negro*, p. 126.

On January 1, 1866, six months after the bank had begun business, Alvord reported, "it has gone into successful operation in nearly all the states South, and promises to do much to instruct and elevate the financial notions of the freedmen. The trustees and friends of the institution believe that the industry of these four millions furnishes a solid basis for its operations. Pauperism can be brought to a close, the freedmen made self-supporting and prosperous, paying for their educational and Christian institutions, and helping to bear the burdens of government by inducing habits of saving in what they earn. That which savings banks have done for the working men of the North it is presumed they are capable of doing for these laborers. I was privately and publicly told that the freedmen welcomed the institution. They understand our explanations of its meaning, and the more intelligent see and appreciate fully its benefits. Calls were made upon me at all large towns for branches of the bank."[9]

Several years later Alvord stated, "the banks are doing more for the people than the schools," which was doubtless quite true, since there were more depositors in the bank than there were children in the much over-rated Bureau schools, and the thrift education given to the holder of the bank book was probably more useful than the kind of education frequently given to the children in the schools.[10] Robert Somers, an

[9] *Ho. Ex. Doc.* No. 70, 39 Cong., 1 Sess.

[10] *Ho. Ex. Doc.*, No. 70, 39 Cong., 1 Sess.; *Ho. Report*, No. 121, 41 Cong., 2 Sess., p. 53; Bradford's Speech in *Cong. Record*, April 22, 1876;

Englishman, who in 1870 and 1871 closely investigated economic conditions in the South, was favorably impressed with the good influence of the bank. He says: "Go in any forenoon and the office is found full of Negroes depositing little sums of money, drawing small sums, or remitting to distant parts of the country where they have relatives to support or debts to discharge. . . . [The literature of the bank] contains an amount of general matter very suitable to the Negroes and very desirable for them to read . . . the Freedmen's Savings and Trust Companies do for the Negroes what our National Savings Banks do for the working classes of England, Scotland, and Ireland. . . . The Negro begins to deposit usually with some special object in view. He wishes to buy a mule or a cow, or a house, or a piece of land, or a shop, or simply to provide a fund against death, sickness, or accident, and pursues his object frequently until it has been accomplished."[11]

THE DEPOSITS AND THE DEPOSITORS

Only those in the vicinity of the larger towns were directly affected by the bank, but the number of depositors within a few years reached a total of 72,000, who were scattered all over the South. About 30,000 of these had deposited sums of $50.00 and under; about 3,000 of them had rather large deposits. The average single deposit in the bank at one time was about $50.00. The average total deposit during the life of the

Ho. Misc. Doc. No. 16, 43 Cong., 2 Sess.; Report of Meigs, National Bank Inspector, Feb. 1874.

[11] Somers, *Southern States*, pp. 54, 55.

bank was $813. Though the bank was established solely for Negroes there were some white depositors. In Charleston nearly 300 of the 2790 depositors were white; at Beaufort there was no other bank, and the whites were permitted to make use of the Negro bank; in New York, where there were 4000 depositors, the 1000 whites were mostly foreigners.

The following statistics[12] will serve to illustrate the workings of the bank:

STATEMENT OF TWO ALABAMA BANKS TO MARCH 31, 1870

	Huntsville Branch	Mobile Branch
Total deposits to March 31, 1870	$89,445.10	$539,534.33
Total number of depositors	500	3,260
Average amount deposited by each	170.89	165.60
Drawn out to March 31, 1870	70,586.60	474,583.60
Balance on March 31, 1870	18,858.50	64,750.83
Average balance due each depositor	47.11	39.82
Spent for land (known)	1,900.00	50,000.00
For seeds, teams, agr. implements	5,000.00	15,000.00
For dwelling houses	800.00	——
For education, books, etc.	1,200.00	——

STATEMENT OF THREE BANKS FOR THE MONTH OF AUGUST, 1872

	Huntsville	Mobile	Montgomery
Deposits for the month	$ 7,343.50	$ 11,136.05	$ 8,522.90
Drafts for the month	10,127.61	18,645.62	8,679.60
Total deposits	416,617.72	1,039,097.05	238,106.80
Total drafts	364,382.51	933,424.30	213,861.71
Total due depositors	52,235.21	105,672.75	24,244.37

The business of the New York City branch to April, 1874, was as follows: Deposits, $3,559,-298.02; drafts, $3,236,981.76.

The following table, compiled from the various

[12] Fleming, *Civil War and Reconstruction in Alabama*, p. 454.

reports of the bank and from the United States public documents, shows the entire business to 1874:

TOTAL BUSINESS OF THE FREEDMEN'S BANK

Year Ending with March	Total Deposits	Deposits Each Year	Balance Due Depositors	Gain Each Year
1866	$ 305,167.00	$ 305,167.00	$ 199,283.42	$ 199,283.42
1867	1,624,853.33	1,319,686.33	366,338.33	167,054.91
1868	3,582,378.36	1,957,535.03	638,338.33	271,960.67
1869	7,257,798.63	3,675,420.27	1,073,465.31	435,166.31
1870	12,605,781.95	5,347,983.32	1,657,006.75	583,541.44
1871	19,592,947.36	7,347,165.41	2,455,836.11	798,827.67
1872	31,260,499.97	11,281,313.06	3,684,739.97	1,227,927.67
1873	——	——	4,200,000.00	——
1874	57,000,000.00	——	3,299,201.00	——

The interest paid on deposits amounted to the sums given in the following table:

INTEREST PAID BY FREEDMEN'S BANK

To January 1, 1867	$ 1,985.47
For 1867	9,521.60
For 1868, to November 1	24,544.08
November 1, 1868 to November 1, 1869	43,896.98
November 1, 1869 to November 1, 1870	59,376.20
November 1, 1870 to November 1, 1871	20,840.32
March 1, 1871 to January 1, 1873	122,215.17

The bank, according to the above showing, had a promising future, and the friends of the Negroes were justified in relying upon it to assist the former slaves to economic freedom. The credit of the institution was rated A-1 to June, 1874, a month before it closed its doors.[13] The strongest branches were located at Augusta, Baltimore, Charleston, Louisville, Memphis, Nashville, New York, Norfolk, Richmond, Savannah, Vicksburg, and Wilmington.

[13] *Ho. Misc. Doc.* No. 16, 43 Cong., 2 Sess., pp. 61, 91; Bruce Report, p. 256; Williams, *History of the Negro Race*, II, 403–411; Hoffman, *Race Traits and Tendencies*, pp. 289, 290.

The deposits in the various branches shortly before the bank was closed in 1874 are shown in the following table: [14]

Branches	Deposits	Branches	Deposits
Alexandria, Va.	$ 21,584	Montgomery, Ala.	$ 29,743
Atlanta, Ga.	28,404	Natchez, Miss.	22,195
Augusta, Ga.	96,882	Nashville, Tenn.	78,525
Baltimore, Md.	303,947	New Bern, N. C.	40,621
Beaufort, S. C.	55,592	New Orleans, La.	240,006
Charleston, S. C.	255,345	New York, N. Y.	344,071
Columbus, Miss.	18,857	Norfolk, Va.	126,337
Columbia, Tenn.	19,823	Philadelphia, Pa.	84,657
Huntsville, Ala.	35,963	Raleigh, N. C.	26,703
Jacksonville, Fla.	22,022	Richmond, Va.	166,000
Lexington, Ky.	34,193	Savannah, Ga.	153,425
Little Rock, Ark.	17,728	Shreveport, La.	30,312
Louisville, Ky.	137,094	Saint Louis, Mo.	58,397
Lynchburg, Va.	19,967	Tallahassee, Fla.	40,207
Macon, Ga.	54,342	Vicksburg, Miss.	104,348
Memphis, Tenn.	56,755	Washington, D. C.	384,789
Mobile, Ala.	96,144	Wilmington, N. C.	45,223

$3,299,201

[14] *Ho. Misc. Doc.* No. 16, 43 Cong., 2 Sess., p. 61.

Chapter V

MISMANAGEMENT AND
OTHER TROUBLES

WEAKNESSES OF THE BANK

NOTWITHSTANDING the popularity of the institution, the rapid accumulation of deposits, and the good intentions of the founders and some of the later officials, there were grave weaknesses in the system, some of which existed almost from the beginning. The trustees were not bound to any responsibility by the charter, nor were they obliged to have a financial interest in the institution; the system was too rapidly expanded, and several branches were established that did not pay expenses; some of the officials were corrupt, and more were inefficient; many Negroes were appointed to positions which they were not competent to hold; the accounts were badly kept, and inspections were infrequent; the connection of the officials of the notorious District of Columbia government with the bank made people suspect corruption; the bank's connection with the Freedmen's Bureau brought discredit upon the former and involved it in politics; the better trustees in disgust withdrew or neglected their duties, and control passed into the hands of the District of Columbia clique; many bad loans were made and

53

the "available" fund was usually invested in very poor securities;[1] the rate of interest—six per cent—paid on deposits was too high; and there was a general shrinkage in real estate values after heavy loans and investments had been made. It will be of interest to examine in detail some of the conditions that undermined the strength of the institution.

Of the thirty-four branches only about half were able to meet expenses regularly, and not until 1872 was the institution as a whole making more than expenses, while even at that date several branches lacked much of being self-supporting. The organization was unwieldy, and the central administration found it difficult to control the branches. Frequently the local cashiers neglected or disobeyed the orders of the inspectors and other higher officials. The establishment of each branch bank necessitated some expenditure of funds, and after the quarters loaned by the Freedmen's Bureau were withdrawn about $170,000 was spent, contrary to the charter, to purchase offices and equipment for the branches. In Washington $260,000 was spent for a banking house. These expenses added to the usual costs of administration and the payment of a high rate of interest on deposits consumed the entire income from the United States securities in which deposits were invested. The branch banks suffered, too, from the hostility of the Negro politician, who was unable to get his hands on the deposits. One of the Negro trustees

[1] Statement of Bank Examiner Meigs in *Sen. Misc. Doc.* No. 88, 43 Cong., 2 Sess.

said that "every colored politician down South was the enemy of the Bank."[2] Robert Somers, the English traveler, after observation of the workings of the bank pointed out in 1870 certain weaknesses and predicted trouble. He called attention to the fact that, although the bank was established under the patronage of the United States government, the latter was not bound to make good any losses; that these would fall upon the depositors alone.[3]

The state governments in the South opposed the operation of the branch banks because they were not under local control, and because they sent money away from the local communities, while the white men's banks were often unfriendly to the objects and methods of the Negro bank. There is evidence that debtors were slower in settling with the Freedmen's Bank than with other banks, that the Freedmen's Bank would get what was left after the others had made choice of what they wanted. Many white men disliked the Freedmen's Bank because they believed that it was connected with the Freedmen's Bureau, and all who disliked the Negro disliked the Negro bank. It was a "race bank," as Frederick Douglass said, and it aroused "race opposition."[4]

There was a persistent belief which came to be shared by depositors, that the bank officials took too much part in southern politics. In 1872 a rumor that funds of the institution were being

[2] Douglas Report, p. 78 (statement of Purvis, of Philadelphia).

[3] Somers, *Southern States*, p. 55.

[4] Douglas Report, pp. 20, 21, 181, 240, 248, 249; *Ho. Ex. Doc.* No. 44, 44 Cong., 1 Sess., p. 5.

used to help elect Grant and to carry the local elections in North Carolina caused a heavy run by the depositors. Another run caused by rumors of the bank's political activities took out half a million dollars. It was practically impossible to keep the institution out of politics, for the Negroes connected with it were natural leaders, and the white officials were frequently in politics through their connection with the Freedmen's Bureau and the local governments.[5]

INACCURATE BOOKKEEPING

The accounts of the bank were never in good shape. This condition was due in part to the inexperience and lack of training of Negro clerks who were gradually employed in place of white clerks. And it was difficult for the management to dismiss an inefficient Negro employee. President Alvord once stated that "the colored people seemed to think that they ought to be employed," and so, too, the management often thought. And in the later years much pressure was brought to bear to get in and keep in as clerks and cashiers prominent Negroes who had little business training. The cashier at Jacksonville did not post the books for six months; other cashiers paid interest on total deposits, not on deposits in hand; few of them could ever make their books balance, and the central office could not force them to keep correct accounts.

The one or two inspectors employed were unable to reach all the branches, for a few which were usually in bad condition kept them busy,

[5] *Ho. Rept.* No. 121, 41 Cong., 2 Sess., p. 51; Douglas Report, p. 78.

while the rest were of necessity neglected. The records in the Washington bank were not much better kept than elsewhere; there was in this city branch only one bookkeeper, who stated that he frequently had to work fourteen hours a day. Such heavy duty was too much for any man— certainly too much for a comparatively inexperienced clerk.

For several years there was a baffling discrepancy of more than $40,000 between the accounts of the branches and those of the principal office. Several times entirely new sets of books were opened in the hope of leaving the past behind and keeping straight for the future. An examination of the books in later years showed that deposits were sometimes entered as withdrawals and *vice versa*; a draft of $31.60 went down on the books as $3,160; $5,300 as $53.00, etc. Sometimes it was impossible to tell from the records whether a certain transaction was a cash payment, an extension of a loan, or a transfer of a loan.[6] One clerk testified that seldom could the books be balanced at night—the error would be from 5 cents to $5,000 one way or the other. When mistakes could not be found, he said, "We always waited for something to turn up"; when the cash balanced, all went out to celebrate the event. Practically all errors before 1871 were errors of ignorance; but after 1871 there was much designed "messing up."

The physical condition of the records was also bad. A committee of experts reported: "We found leaves cut from the original ledger, leaves

[6]Report of accountants, Bruce Report, pp. 174, 282.

without number pasted together, balances not brought forward . . . original entries do not conform to the meaning of the transaction when carried to the ledger—credits posted as debits," and so on.[7] Once when the headquarters office had several of the volumes rebound, the binders in trimming the edges cut off lines of figures.

The Douglas Committee in 1876 called the attention of Congress to the condition of the books. "Their condition," the committee report stated, "indicates a settled purpose, running through a series of years, to muddle and confuse accounts so as to make them unintelligible. But whether through design or not, such is the result. If nothing more than an occasional mistake or slight irregularity occurred, it might be set down, perhaps, to the inexperience of the bookkeepers or the want of clerical force to write up the books properly, without imputing very great harm to anyone. But it is far otherwise. The books are mutilated and defaced—leaves cut out in some places and firmly pasted together in others— without proper indexes to guide and direct the searcher into the hidden mysteries—abounding in false entries and forced balances, altogether exhibiting a labyrinth of winding and never-ending perplexities and contradictions that defy the scrutiny of the sharpest experts."[8]

INCOMPETENT CASHIERS

Serious troubles were due also to the inexperi-

[7] Bruce Report, pp. 31, 163, 164, 230–233, 243, 244, 246, 250, 256, 269 (Testimony of A. M. Sperry, O. O. Howard, Stickney, C. A. Fleetwood, Tomkins, Augusta); Reports of Experts, March 7, 1876; Douglass, *Life and Times,* p. 487.

[8] *Ho. Repor*' No. 502, 44 Cong., 1 Sess.

ence and ignorance of cashiers at the branches.
They had not always the courage to refuse re-
quests for favors made by influential men, and
from the beginning certain favored individuals
were frequently permitted to overdraw their
accounts. Before 1870 when loans were forbidden the prohibition could be avoided by allowing
overdrafts. Although in the long run not a great
deal was lost in this way, in many instances it
was quite difficult to secure the payment of this
money when it was badly needed. The Negro
officials were sometimes over-persuaded by a
certain strenuous kind of speculator, such as
Vandenburg, the District of Columbia public
works contractor, who usually managed to make
"Daddy" Wilson, the Negro cashier in Washington, allow his overdrafts even when Wilson had
positive instructions not to permit such favors.
It was easier at some places for a white man to
borrow money than for a Negro, and many
whites secured loans on too easy terms. Churches
which were in debt also found the Freedmen's
Bank a too considerate creditor.

After the charter was amended in 1870,[9] the
cashiers at the principal branches were permitted
to make loans on real estate. This amendment
of the charter was designed to overcome the
many objections to the original policy of the
bank in gathering deposits all over the South
while lending or investing mainly in the District
of Columbia. As soon as the cashiers were given
authority to make loans, they were besieged by
a dangerous class of borrowers, who would have

[9] See Appendix, p. 136.

received scant consideration at the ordinary bank. In scores of cases loans were made without any real security whatever, and second mortgage paper was frequently accepted. This practice was gradually checked and was stopped in most of the branches in 1872. But since public sentiment favored the lending of money in the community, deposits began to dwindle as soon as local loans were forbidden.

The law of 1870, requiring that loans be made only on real estate valued at double the amount of the loan, was often violated, and the cashiers proceeded to make investments on their own responsibility. Some of them loaned funds against the nearly worthless scrip or bonds issued by the carpetbag state and local governments; others loaned on cotton; some even made loans on perishable crops. The Jacksonville branch put out money on nearly everything that was offered, from sawmills located in the Florida swamps to shadowy claims on property in the city. Several branch banks, notably Beaufort and Jacksonville, began to go into the regular banking business, and, with a few others, endeavored to act somewhat independently of the central office.[10]

CASES OF FRAUD

Not only were the cashiers sometimes incompetent and disregardful of laws, regulations, and business principles, but several of them were personally guilty of defrauding the institution

[10] Bruce Report, p. 28; Douglas Report, pp. 25, 39, 48, 49; C. A. Meigs, Report, in *Ho. Misc. Doc.* No. 16, 43 Cong., 2 Sess., p. 66; 14 Florida Reports (1874), pp. 418–434.

or its depositors. Most of the inefficient officials, it seems, were Negroes; most of the dishonest ones were white. There was a belief, often expressed after the failure of the bank, that when a white cashier had embezzled the funds and involved the accounts of a branch, a Negro official would be put in his place to serve as a scapegoat when exposure came.

The white clergymen who were cashiers proved to be quite unable to withstand the temptations offered by the presence of the cash in the vaults. Purvis, one of the trustees, afterwards asserted, "The cashiers at most of the branches were a set of scoundrels and thieves—and made no bones about it—but they were all pious men, and some of them were ministers. The cashier at Jacksonville was a minister and today he has a large Sunday school; almost all of them are ministers." Cashier Hamilton at Lexington, Kentucky, a graduate of Oberlin, was also a preacher and a Sunday school superintendent. He did not steal from the bank itself, but from the depositors by drawing out on forged checks the money of those who seldom came in with their pass books.

Several of the cashiers endeavored to build up a banking business for whites as well as for blacks, planning ultimately to turn their branch banks into regular banks, state or national. Charges were made that Rev. Philip D. Cory, cashier at Atlanta, discouraged Negro depositors in order to secure white ones; that he wanted a "white man's" bank. On this account the Negroes were opposed to him and the Atlanta branch did not thrive. Finally, in 1874, he was removed, and a Negro put in his place. The latter discovered that Cory had embezzled about $10,000 of the deposits, and had him prosecuted in the state courts of Georgia, where he was sentenced to four years in prison—the only accused person connected with the Freedmen's Bank who was ever punished. Cory finally made a compromise: The prosecution was to allow him to be pardoned in order to accept an appointment as Indian agent out West, and from the proceeds of this office he promised to repay what he had stolen. Hamilton, the Lexington embezzler, was also allowed to accept an Indian agency.[11] The headquarters officials testified in later years that when attempts were made to punish defaulting cashiers it was difficult to secure a conviction in the local courts.

The cashiers taken over from the Freedmen's Bureau gave more than a fair proportion of the trouble. The two in Alabama were typical. At Mobile the cashier, C. A. Woodward, was charged with appropriating to his own use $3,375 which, he stated, the Freedmen's Bureau owed to him. At Montgomery, Edwin Beecher, the cashier, made investments, contrary to regulations, of about $20,000 in securities that proved to be valueless, and for several years afterwards carried a shortage of $18,000 on his books. Finally the headquarters authorities secured a bond from him and sold him the business, but he failed and the amount of the bond was not collected.

The Beaufort branch was on a peculiar basis,

[11] Douglas Report, pp. 2, 4, 25, 71, 77, 78, 260; Bruce Report, p. 31.

with problems all its own. From the beginning, when Saxton's military bank was absorbed into the Freedmen's Bank, the cashier, Scovel, had endeavored to run things to suit himself. By repeated dispensations from headquarters he became almost independent of the central administration, and proceeded to do a regular banking business. He wanted to transform his branch into a national bank, and the trustees at Washington decided to allow him to do so, since there was no other bank in the town and the white merchants were anxious to secure banking facilities. But the inspectors soon found that there had been an embezzlement at Beaufort of at least $10,000, and that bad investments had caused a loss of many thousands more. At one time it was supposed that the loss would reach $100,000.[12]

The officials of the Washington branch bank were frequently under fire of the press. "Daddy" Wilson, a Negro, was cashier, and Boston, his son-in-law, was assistant cashier. Both lived in style beyond their means, and repeatedly it was charged that they were using the funds of the depositors. But with one exception there were no instances of embezzlement proved against them. Most of the attacks on their management simply assumed that Wilson and Boston were the dupes of more cunning thieves. The following is an example of the publicity they secured:

"Old Daddy Wilson stands about 5 feet 10 inches in his boots, is square built, solemn, the color of polished coal tar, and sports gold spec-

[12] Bruce Report, pp. 247, 248.

tacles . . . Brother Boston, young, airy, dressed
in the height of fashion, and the color of Java
coffee, moves lightly among the dingy and di-
lapidated customers . . . Boston is fond of
finery and fond of showing it. Finery and high
sounding words are Boston's weakness. . . .
Daddy Wilson got his wisdom in financial matters by keeping a little nick-nack shop on Fif-
teenth Street. Daddy Wilson and Brother Boston are mere figure-heads kept there in dumb
show by cunning fellows who work the machinery from behind the scenes and are filling their
own pockets."[13]

The one case of fraud proved against the two
was a small and mean one. Boston had been
"borrowing" small sums from an ignorant depositor named Watkins, without giving security,
Watkins for his part thinking that none was
necessary. Boston had also been checking out
Watkins' money without the knowledge of the
latter, who could not read his pass book. Wilson,
the cashier, allowed this practice and paid the
money to Boston, so that in this way about
$1,000 was stolen before Watkins discovered it.
His losses were far greater than the losses of the
average sufferer, but over the South many
others had similar experiences. The following
account from Watkins' deposition may be taken
as typical of the feelings of thousands of Negroes
who lost their money:

About a week after the bank closed [1874] I carried my
passbook up there, and also my little boy's. My little boy
had $60 in the bank, I think, and I had nine hundred odd.

[13] Savannah *Morning News*, Dec. 9, 1871; in Washington *Patriot*,
Dec. 13, 1871.

I wanted to find out how I stood. I saw Boston about fifteen or sixteen times after the bank closed, and I waited and waited and waited, till at last I went to the bank to see about my book. I could not find Boston in, but I said to the clerk there, "Do you know how Watkins' account is?" He looked at the book and said, "Yes, you have 40 cents." I said, "Forty hells." He said, "Yes." Said I, "What will I do?" Said he, "I don't know." I said I never had any money and asked him to tell me where I could find Boston. He told me where to find Boston, somewhere on "E" Street, below the Patent office, and there I found Boston. I went in and commenced pulling off my coat to fight him right away. I said, "Boston, what is the meaning of this that I have only forty cents in the bank." His face got white and said he, "Mr. Watkins, I drew it out." "Hell," said I, "you drew it out and told me nothing about it?" "Well," said he, "I will fix that all right." The bank was to pay a dividend in two or three weeks' time, and he said, "I will pay you a dividend on the 15th of next month." Said I, "Jesus Christ, I do not know what to do with you." The clerk at the bank showed me the checks on which the money was drawn, but, of course, I did not know one check from the other . . . I could not get anything out of Boston. . . .

[Before the bank was closed] I said, "Mr. Wilson, I don't want to get closed up in this concern. A man in this town unless he has money, is not worth more than a dog. I have worked hard night and day, for this money, and so has my wife, and it should not be closed up in this way." He said, "You see that Treasury over there, don't you?" I said, "Yes." "Well," said he, "there is no more chance of this bank closing or bursting than there is of that Treasury." I said, "If that is so, it is all right." He said, "It is just prejudice that white people have got against us." Then I made myself contented. My heart went down and I went to work. There the matter stood, and only 40 cents on my pass book to my credit. They did not rob my boy's book. When I was loaning money to Boston, I supposed it was all right as he was cashier of the bank. I supposed he owned it all himself. I did not know. . . .

Question. I understand you to say that this money was the joint earnings of yourself and wife?

Answer. Yes; she took in washing, and worked day and night, every day for the whole year. I have never been to a picnic or a ball since I have been in town."[14]

The table below gives the list of branches where shortages were discovered by the inspectors before the failure of the bank.[15]

SHORTAGE AT THE BRANCH BANKS

Branch	Cashier	Shortage
Atlanta	Cory	$ 8,000
Beaufort	Scovel	{ 10,000 / 100,000
Mobile	Woodward	3,375
New Bern	Nelson	1,250
Wilmington	McCumber	3,000
Natchez	Jordan	1,125
Jacksonville	Coon	{ 100,000 / 10,000
Nashville	Cary	1,000
Vicksburg	Lee	11,000
Lynchburg	Bronough	900
Lexington, Ky.	Hamilton	5,000
Montgomery	Beecher	{ 29,000 / 18,000

It is not possible to ascertain from the records exactly how large the shortages were at Beaufort, Jacksonville, and Montgomery; in the table the smallest and largest estimates are given. There were shortages at other branches than those named above, but they were adjusted. It is probable that much of the deficit at the honestly managed branches was due to poor bookkeeping, too large payments of interest, unnecessary expenses, and inexperienced clerks.

NEGLECTFUL AND UNFAITHFUL TRUSTEES

Another cause of weakness was the gradual

[14] *Ho. Report* No. 502, 44 Cong., 1 Sess., p. 29.
[15] Douglas Report, p. 5.

deterioration of the governing body. The original board of trustees was composed principally of men of high character, several of them noted for business ability, and as long as the central office was in New York a sufficient number attended the meetings to keep the business going properly. But after the removal of headquarters to Washington many trustees found it impossible to attend the meetings and thus through non-service most of the better members were in time eliminated. The honest and efficient trustees, like Ketchum of New York and Stewart of Baltimore, were opposed to the management of the bank after headquarters were removed to Washington, but as they were unable to reform it they resigned. Ketchum was one of the last of the trustees who took an intelligent and helpful interest in the bank, but he finally resigned as a protest against the Seneca loan business.[16]

Since it was difficult to fill the vacant places on the board of trustees with men of standing and experience, it came about that the majority of those elected were put in merely to fill up the lists. They had slight capacity, frequently no business connections, and but little property; the main qualification was to have some kind of a record as an abolitionist, or as a Freedmen's Bureau official, or as a friend of the freedmen. Too many of them took little interest in the business. Queer characters were put in as "dummies," and it was found later that some of them had never read the act of incorporation of the bank.

[16] See below, p. 77.

The incapable ones were controlled by the few
efficient ones who, after 1869–1870, were the
District of Columbia members. The latter
formed a kind of "ring" for their mutual benefit,
and were involved in financial operations that
made their connection with the Freedmen's
Bank of considerable value to them. They were
at once officials of the bank, and officers of the
Bureau, or of the army, or of the government
of the District of Columbia, and some were interested in corporations which wished to borrow
from the bank. The two Howards, Balloch,
Whittlesey, Alvord, and Smith were Freedmen's
Bureau officials and were connected with Howard University, and with other extensive borrowers; Cooke[17] and Huntington were officials
in the First National Bank, which unloaded some
of its bad loans upon the Freedmen's Bank;
Cooke, Eaton, Huntington, Balloch, and Richards were connected with firms[18] that borrowed
large sums, notwithstanding the fact that officials of the bank were prohibited by law from
borrowing from it, directly or indirectly. Several
were also connected with the Building Block
Company of Freedmen's Bureau fame. There
was hardly an officer after 1871 who was not
connected with some outside interest that borrowed from the bank.[19]

The trustees were under no bonds to secure

[17] Henry D. Cooke, brother of Jay Cooke, was the first territorial
governor of the District of Columbia (1871–1873).—*National Cyc. Biog.*,
X, 510; *Cyclopedia Amer. Biog.*; Oberholtzer, *Jay Cooke*, II, 556.

[18] For example, the Seneca Sandstone Company and the Metropolitan
Paving Company.

[19] See Peirce, *Freedmen's Bureau*, pp. 117, 123.

proper execution of their trust, and were not required to make any deposit in the bank. The law fixed as a quorum nine out of fifty trustees, and further required the affirmative vote of at least five of the nine on money matters. But the trustees provided in the by-laws for a finance committee of five to pass upon loans, of whom three should be a quorum. Thus three officials could and did habitually dispose of financial business when the law required at least nine. Often two members of the committee, or one, or even the actuary (cashier) negotiated important loans without reference to the trustees. Sometimes the actuary made a loan and then hunted up three members of the finance committee to sign the proper papers. Vice-president Clephane testified that the actuary sometimes came to him and said, "I am going to count you present," although Clephane had not been at the finance committee meeting. As he said, "We left [the making of loans] very much to the actuary to examine into. We were apt to take his representation of things."

When at last the rank and file of the trustees began to realize that they were being used as dummies, the sharpers who had been managing them resigned and left them to flounder about in their own confusion. Alvord, the president after 1868, was probably honest throughout, but he was weak and old and at one time was so deranged mentally that he had to be sent to a sanitarium. The finance committee refused to allow him a vote on measures that came before them. He could only preside. But he was kept in office on account of his popularity among the Negroes.

The actuaries, first Eaton, and later Stickney, the nephew of Eaton, conducted business very much as they pleased, and as the speculators inside and outside wanted them to do. As a token of the regard in which he was held by the speculators who borrowed money from the bank, Eaton possessed a number of shares, which cost him nothing, in one of the various public works companies of the District. A great deal of the bad paper held by the bank bore Eaton's endorsement.[20]

THE AMENDMENT TO THE CHARTER

The hoarded deposits of the Freedmen's Bank having attracted attention of the speculators in Washington, an amendment to the charter was secured in 1870 by those of the trustees who were in sympathy with a more active loan and investment policy. The amendment merely provided that one half of that portion of the deposits formerly invested in United States securities might be invested in notes and bonds secured by mortgage on real estate of at least twice the value of the loan. The bank was also authorized to improve the real estate that it already held, provided that none of the principal of the deposits should be used. The inference is that the bank was already holding property in violation of the original charter, which permitted no investments in real estate. The $260,000 spent on

[20] Bruce Report, pp. 51, 58, 109, 110, 119, 178, 222; Douglas Report, pp. 36, 89, 91, 95.

a headquarters building and $170,000 paid for property at branches was illegally taken from the principal of the deposits, for only in 1872 was the annual income really sufficient to pay running expenses and interest on deposits.

The amendment was secured principally through the efforts of one of the finance committee, W. S. Huntington, who was cashier of the First National Bank[21] and who belonged to the District of Columbia ring. The reasons for the changes, as given before a committee of Congress, were: (1) That the United States debt would probably soon be refunded at a lower rate of interest and that the bank could not then get a sufficient income from its investments in bonds; (2) that money was worth more than 5 per cent, and that unless the bank paid at least 6 per cent interest on deposits the freedmen would place their funds elsewhere. Consequently the bank must make more money. It was claimed, particularly in the South whence came most of the deposits, that there was a general demand for loans and that a high rate of interest could be secured. It was also asserted that the new arrangement would enable the bank to continue the 6 per cent rate of interest on deposits and would satisfy those depositors who thought that "the money ought to stay at home," while under present conditions the Negroes regarded the branch banks as a "drag net" to bring the money into Washington.[22]

Representative Cook, of Ohio, introduced the

[21] See Oberholtzer, *Jay Cooke, passim.*
[22] *Ho. Misc. Doc.* No. 16, 43 Cong., 2 Sess., p. 66.

proposed amendment in the House, where it passed without discussion. In the upper house Senator Cameron of Pennsylvania vigorously objected to the amendment on the ground that it would endanger the funds, which were evidently now in the hands of irresponsible persons, that speculation and loss would certainly result, and that the bank would be destroyed. Those who were interested in securing the amendment stirred up the leading Negroes to remonstrate with Cameron, who said: "If they want to be cheated I will make no more trouble." He then ceased his objection, and the bill became law.[23]

Within three years Cameron's predictions were fulfilled. As soon as possible every cent that the institution could command was loaned to private individuals and corporations. The law requiring that the real estate be twice the value of the loan was usually disregarded. Kilbourn and Latta, agents of a real estate combine and large borrowers from the bank, were appointed as its appraisers of real estate. Loans were made rapidly and recklessly, on bills against the District government, on District securities issued without warrant of law, on second mortgages, on stock in promotion companies, and on other paper of doubtful value. The resources of the bank were soon tied up in loans of such a character that it was practically impossible to realize upon them without long delay.[24]

[23] *Cong. Globe*, March 21, April 15, 28, and May 2, 1870, pp. 2095, 2726, 2732, 2738, 3038, 3064, 3147, 3344; Douglas Report, pp. 37, 38; *The Nation*, April 5, 1875. See Appendix, p. 136.

[24] Even before 1870, $84,340.67 had been loaned on real estate, contrary to the law.—Bruce Report, p. 288.

LOANS TO SPECULATORS

The local District of Columbia spoilsmen found a mine in the bank. Vandenburg, a public works contractor, secured a loan of $30,000 without any security except the verbal indorsement of A. R. Shepherd,[25] the District "Boss." Vandenburg failed to pay, and Shepherd after delay made good the loan, but took occasion to remind Stickney, the actuary, that "if you do business in that kind of a loose way you are a damned fool."

The management seemed unable to refuse loans to the favored contractors and speculators of the District. Vandenburg loaded the bank with bills against the District which he was unable to collect. In all he secured loans amounting to $180,000, of which about $150,000 was still due when the bank failed. Several promotion companies in which he was interested also secured large sums resulting in a final loss to the bank of about $50,000. As one of the officials said: "Vandenburg got what he wanted; couldn't keep him from getting it."[26]

JAY COOKE AND THE FIRST NATIONAL BANK

The Freedmen's Bank was utilized by other banks to carry questionable paper for them, to

[25] Alexander Robey Shepherd (1835–1902) was a local District of Columbia politician, who was prominent in helping to get a measure through Congress in 1871 providing for the establishment of a territorial government for the District of Columbia. When H. D. Cooke, the first territorial governor resigned in 1873 Shepherd was appointed governor. Charges of corruption were brought against him, and in 1874 Congress abolished the territorial government. The District was then placed under three commissioners. President Grant nominated Shepherd to be one of the commissioners but the Senate refused to confirm him.—*Cyclopedia of American Biography.*

[26] Douglas Report, pp. 76, 77, 91; Bruce Report, p. 161.

finance doubtful enterprises, and to furnish
cheap loans. Jay Cooke and Company, the fi-
nanciers, through their control of the finance
committee, were able to borrow $500,000 at one
time paying only 5 per cent interest, while the
Freedmen's Bank was paying 6 per cent to
depositors on the same money.[27]

Between 1870 and 1873 the Freedmen's Bank
was practically controlled by Jay Cooke and
Company and the First National Bank. It suffered much under this control. H. D. Cooke and
W. S. Huntington, president and cashier respectively, of the First National Bank of Washington, were trustees of the Freedmen's Bank and
members of its finance committee. When Cooke's
bank made a bad transaction, these men used
their position and influence to transfer the poor
securities to the Freedmen's Bank. They also
used the latter as a dumping ground for the bad
private claims of themselves and friends. Huntington lived in a house belonging to one R. P.
Dodge and, in order to get his rent reduced,
negotiated for Dodge a $13,000 loan from his
own (the First National) bank. This bank held
Dodge's notes until they were due and then
through Huntington's influence with Eaton, the
actuary, transferred the paper to the Freedmen's
Bank. After Huntington died Dodge was asked
to pay but objected on the ground that the
money from the loan went to Huntington, not
to himself. Stickney, the actuary who succeeded
Eaton, said of Huntington, "If he wanted to
have anything done, it was done." Trustees

[27] Douglas Report, pp. 8, 11, 12; Bruce Report, p. 179.

and finance committee seemed unable to check him.[28]

PROCEDURE IN MAKING LOANS

The charter required a reserve of one third of the deposits as an available fund for immediate use. This was to be kept in the bank or on deposit in other banks. But after the amendment of the charter in 1870 the actuary, counselled by the finance committee, used this fund for general banking purposes, and soon had the whole of it tied up in miscellaneous loans and investments of poor character. It was said later that no paper was so worthless that it would not pass at the Freedmen's Bank if it had some trustee or friend of a trustee behind it. Loans were made on individual notes endorsed by trustees who had no deposits in the bank and no property in sight and who under the law should not have endorsed any paper accepted by the bank.

An example of trustee action in regard to loans may be seen in the case of Zalmon Richards, a trustee, who had an accommodating custom of endorsing the notes of borrowers, and who was finally ruined because of this practice. After the failure of the bank, Richards came before the Congressional investigating committee to testify about conditions. Richards did not know anything about the business of the bank or the requirements of its charter, yet he had been a prominent trustee. The following extract from his testimony will serve to illustrate his com-

[28] Bruce Report, p. 161; Douglas Report, p. 77.

fortable lack of a sense of responsibility and also his notions of business:

Mr. Richards: I know that judgment was taken against me as an indorser, and I am free to say that if the Lord ever puts money enough into my pocket I will pay it.

The Chairman (Senator Bruce): The Lord will not do it for you. You must do it yourself in some way.

Mr. Richards: Well, the Lord may help me to do it. I have got a good deal of confidence in the Lord yet.

The Chairman: The Lord, Mr. Richards, doubtless is engaged in more profitable business than putting money in your pockets.[29]

Sometimes no collateral of any kind was put up. Eaton, the first actuary, formed the habit of making loans and investments without consulting the finance committee. These he reported as "cash" or as "available."[30] As Stickney, the second actuary, said, the available fund soon became "very unavailable." Much of it was finally lost, for out of it the most unsafe loans were made.

It was often the case that those who borrowed and those who negotiated the loans on the part of the bank were practically identical persons. Trustees and officials were members of companies that borrowed from the bank, or sold to it doubtful securities. Cooke, Huntington, Clephane, Eaton, Howard, and Balloch were prominent among those who borrowed from the bank in which they were officials. Howard University, the Y. M. C. A., and several churches and schools were able to borrow because of the connection of members of their governing bodies with the bank. The Seneca Sandstone Company

[29] Bruce Report, pp. 129–136.

[30] Douglas Report, pp. 67, 91, 149; Bruce Report, pp. 27, 140, 282.

and the First National Bank, both large borrowers from the Freedmen's Bank, had representatives on the finance committee of the latter
institution. H. D. Cooke, the First National
Bank representative, when later called before
investigating committees, professed profound
ignorance of all the questionable transactions.[31]

Balloch, a trustee and member of the finance
committee, made a bad private loan in 1870,
and in 1872 transferred his claim to the bank.[32]
Huntington of the First National Bank borrowed $3,000 for one day and never repaid it.[33]
Eaton, the actuary, was given by Vandenburg
one-half interest in a $100,000 sewer-pipe con-
tract to reward him for his kindness in securing
loans for said Vandenburg.[34] Balloch borrowed
$2,000 in 1872, giving as collateral $2,000 in
United States five per cent bonds. Later these
bonds were withdrawn and $1,800 in less valu-
able railroad securities were substituted.[35] There
was a loss of $32,000 caused by frequent loans
to R. I. Fleming who, it was well known, was
practically bankrupt. As security he offered bills
against the District of Columbia, Y. M. C. A.
bonds, and other doubtful paper.

THE SENECA SANDSTONE COMPANY

As examples to show the character of loans
made after 1870 and to illustrate the business

[31] Douglas Report, pp. 8, 9, 76, 77, 91, 93; Bruce Report, pp. 51,
110, 111; Savannah *News*, Dec. 9, 1871.
[32] Bruce Report, p. 176.
[33] Douglas Report, p. 176.
[34] Douglas Report, p. 12.
[35] Bruce Report, p. 153.

methods of the authorities there may be mentioned the loans made to Evan Lyons and to the Seneca Sandstone Company. Lyons, who owned 60 acres of land in Washington County, Maryland, repeatedly applied for small loans. Four times he was refused by the finance committee, because it was believed that his title to the land was not clear. Finally he secured a loan of $34,000—more than the property was worth. The facts that came out upon investigation were as follows: Lyons' land was already covered with mortgages which he could not raise. As his creditors wanted the money, it was agreed that they should give up their first mortgage claims on the property, take second mortgages, and allow Lyons to secure a large loan from the Freedmen's Bank under a first mortgage. This was done; the creditors and Lyons divided the proceeds and left the bank with the land, on which it lost $25,000.[36] There is evidence to show that other creditors used this method to get money back from bad loans. When the debtor and the creditor got together the bank was helpless, especially when its appraiser happened to be interested in the transaction.

The Seneca Sandstone transaction was never fully cleared up, but the principal facts that were ascertained upon investigation were as follows: The Maryland Freestone Mining and Manufacturing Company, commonly called the Seneca Sandstone Company, was a promising enterprise, incorporated in 1867 with such men as General Grant, Secretary Seward, and Caleb Cushing as

[36] Bruce Report, report of Committee, and pp. 124, 154.

stockholders. In 1868 Cooke and Huntington of the First National Bank, both trustees of the Freedmen's Bank, secured control of the company, over-capitalized it, declared a stock dividend to the original incorporators, issued a lot of first and second mortgage bonds, which were placed on sale, and then speculation began.[37]

As the Freedmen's Bank offered an easy mark, from it a loan of $51,000 was secured in 1871, and $49,000 in second mortgage bonds and $20,000 in first mortgage bonds were given as collateral.[38] The second mortgage bonds were generally known to be valueless, and, the fact of the loan becoming public, attacks were made by the newspapers upon the bank management.[39] Thereupon Eaton, the actuary, went to Kilbourn and Evans, real estate brokers and appraisers for the bank, and made an agreement with them and with the Seneca Sandstone Company to change the form of the loan and thus protect the finance committee from hostile criticism. The account of the Seneca Company was then closed, the loan being transferred on the books to Kilbourn and Evans, who gave their joint note,

[37] The property of the Seneca Sandstone Company cost $120,000; the company was incorporated with a capital stock of $500,000, later raised to $1,000,000, and a stock dividend of $300,000 was declared. Not more than enough money was collected from stockholders to pay the original cost of the property. It was charged that noted men received blocks of stock free in return for the use of their names, but the charge was not proved. See Douglas and Bruce Reports, *passim.*

[38] An earlier transaction in 1870 was the "loan" of $18,000 upon $20,000 first mortgage Seneca bonds, but it was testified that there was no intention on either side of redeeming the bonds—they were to be considered an investment.

[39] It was charged that loans secured by collateral of this kind were in violation of the charter of the bank. It was at this time that Ketchum, of the board of trustees, after objecting in vain to such loans, resigned.

payable in six months, supported by good collateral plus the second mortgage collateral of the
first loan.

So far the transaction seemed good business,
but at the same time a curious secret agreement
was made by the bank officials with Kilbourn
and Evans, securing the latter against loss. This
agreement was signed for the finance committee
by Huntington (of the Seneca Company, etc.),
Clephane, and Tuttle, and by Eaton, the actuary. It recited the list of the securities (including
$75,000 in second mortgage Seneca bonds) pur-
porting to have been deposited by Kilbourn and
Evans, and stated that in case Kilbourn and
Evans did not pay the note at maturity, their
note and all their own collateral securities were
to be returned to them except the $75,000 in
second mortgage Seneca bonds. It was understood that the transaction was not to make Kilbourn and Evans responsible in any way; they
were simply allowing the use of their names as a
temporary accommodation. In other words the
bank was to pay $51,000 for $75,000 in unsalable
bonds.

Two years later, in 1873, the note and securities were surrendered according to agreement,
and only the $75,000 in second mortgage bonds
was left to secure the bank against loss. The
actuary early in 1874 closed the Kilbourn and
Evans account and again charged the Seneca
Company with the $51,000 and with $7,500 ac-
crued interest. The $20,000 first mortgage bonds
held from the Seneca Company had disappeared
in 1872 in a transaction in which Kidwell, then

president of the Seneca Company, purchased them from Eaton for $20,580, but if this money was paid the bank's record did not show it. The Seneca Company also secured money through individuals who borrowed on second mortgage Seneca bonds and then turned the proceeds over to the company.[40]

The responsible authorities, of course, professed to have little or no knowledge of these transactions. Tuttle, a member of the finance committee, who was a United States treasury official, said that he did not read the Kilbourn and Evans agreement before signing it, and he further stated that he never read any papers presented for his signature. He thus explained: "I said that I wanted at least two names to precede mine and that I wanted the actuary's name so as to know that it was all right. . . . I always told them that they must not deceive me." This to Cooke and Huntington![41] In several transactions there was so much swapping and juggling of securities that the authorities of the Freedmen's Bank became confused and lost themselves in the confusion.

RESULTS OF MISMANAGEMENT

Such was the mismanagement that resulted in the failure of the Freedmen's Bank. In 1873 the available fund was no longer available, the

[40] The report of the Bruce Committee gives a full account of the Seneca business. See also Bruce Report, pp. 52, 55, 91–97, 141–144, 178, 201–210, 283. Douglas Report, pp. 31, 74–76, 104. For details in regard to other loans see Bruce Report, for the facts about those made to Kennedy, Fleming, First Baptist Church, Y. M. C. A., Howard University, etc.

[41] Douglas Report, p. 104.

depositors had become alarmed, and three serious runs had been made within eighteen months which reduced the deposits by $1,800,000. Business depression came, real estate declined in value, the bank could realize on few of its securities, and the bad loans could not be called. Jay Cooke and Company and the First National Bank failed, and, in order to pass the crisis, the Freedmen's Bank had to sacrifice its best securities and also borrow at ruinous rates. While the "runs" were going on some of the trustees and officers removed their own accounts. It was understood among the officials that each would look after the others' "safety" in case of a disastrous run.[42]

These "runs" came just as the deposits became large enough to pay the expenses of the bank. They were caused by rumors of the use of funds for political purposes and by newspaper criticism of the management and policy of the institution. As a result of the heavy withdrawals the authorities were forced to require the depositors to give sixty days or more notice before drawing out deposits. This action, though legal and provided for in the regulations, did much to destroy the now uneasy confidence of the Negroes, and few additional deposits were made during the latter part of 1873 and in 1874.[43] The Comptroller of the Currency reported in 1873 that there was serious mismanagement in the affairs of the bank, and in February, 1874, a national bank

[42] Bruce Report, pp. 78, 181, 222.

[43] I have been unable to ascertain how much was deposited after March, 1873.

examiner's report showed that the institution had actually been insolvent for a year.[44] But for several weeks the conclusions of this report were not generally known.

When the bank began to show signs of weakness the few trustees and officials who had money on deposit withdrew it, while at the same time the management tried to evade investigation by Congress, and to delude the Negroes into making more deposits. Some of those most interested in the welfare of the institution, among whom was Sperry, endeavored in 1873–1874 to secure an investigation by Congress. But somehow it developed that anyone who expressed doubt of the bank's policy was suspected of hostility to the Negro race. President Alvord and the trustees were also opposed to any investigation. This attitude was, on the part of most of them, due probably to ignorance of actual conditions. Sperry was of the opinion that an investigation by Congress, if it had been made in time, would have saved the bank, but he said, "We could not get the help from Congress at the time we needed it."[45]

During the runs the trustees neglected the affairs of the bank; only one of them—Purvis, a Negro—came in to advise and assist the actuary, who during the crisis had to act most of the time on his own responsibility. The clique of speculators had resigned in good time and left affairs to the well-meaning incompetents and the Ne-

[44] Douglas Report, p. 180; Meig's reports in Report of Comptroller of the Currency, 1873–1874.

[45] Douglas Report, pp. 254–256; Bruce Report, pp. 178, 179, 238.

groes. A faction of the trustees, dissatisfied with
Alvord's mismanagement, now determined to
bring about a change by electing Frederick
Douglass to the presidency in the hope that he
would restore confidence and reform abuses.[46]

The report of the national bank examiner
brought matters to a crisis. The examiner, C. A.
Meigs, reported that on January 24, 1874, the
nominal resources of the Freedmen's Bank were
valued at $3,121,101.00 and that its liabilities
amounted to $3,338,896.15. So there was a defi-
cit of at least $217,886.15 and the depositors
could hope to get back not more than 93 cents
on the dollar, even if the securities held by the
bank were sound. The examiner ascribed the
condition of the bank to several causes: there
were, he said, too many non-paying branches;
cashiers had been given too much authority in
making loans and had made many bad ones; too
high interest—six per cent—was paid on deposits; during the runs the best securities had
been sacrificed; and finally there was the careless
bookkeeping, and the poor investments made in
the District of Columbia.[47]

[46] Bruce Report, pp. 163–165, 181, 183, 254, 255, 256; Douglas Report, pp. 17, 76, 178, 179, 180; Douglass, *Life and Times*, pp. 488, *et seq.*

[47] Report of C. A. Meigs to Comptroller of the Currency, Feb. 14,
1874, in *Ho. Misc. Doc.* No. 16, 43 Cong., 2 Sess.

Chapter VI

THE ADMINISTRATION OF
FREDERICK DOUGLASS.
THE COLLAPSE OF THE BANK

FREDERICK DOUGLASS MADE PRESIDENT

TESTIFYING before the Douglas Committee in 1876, Dr. Purvis, a Negro member of the board of trustees, explained why Frederick Douglass was made president. "Prior to the last election in March, 1874," he said, "we had determined to get rid of an element which we believed to be the cause of all our disasters, and we colored men put into the Bank Mr. Douglass. We looked upon Mr. Alvord as old and incompetent."[1] The testimony of others before the Douglas Committee and the Bruce Committee shows that for various reasons nearly all concerned were willing for Douglass to be made president and for several of the District of Columbia trustees to be replaced by others. Some, looking for a scapegoat, were anxious that colored officials be in charge when the bank failed as they were sure it would; others thought that a Negro administration would restore the confidence of the depositors and enable the institution to survive until better times.

Douglass was elected president in March,

[1] Douglas Report, p. 76.

1874, and assumed office in April. He stated afterwards that he accepted the presidency, not because he had any experience in banking, but because he thought that his influence with his own race would strengthen the institution and enable it to weather the storm. Both Alvord, the outgoing president, and Stickney, the actuary, assured him, he said, that the bank was sound. Alvord knew no better, and probably Stickney hoped that it would pull through. Alvord then accepted the presidency of the ill-famed Seneca Sandstone Company, in order, he said, to recover the amount due the bank.[2]

Douglass, when he took charge, knew little of the previous mismanagement of the business, and some of the officials, especially Stickney, took care to keep him in ignorance of actual conditions. So he was without difficulty induced to issue circulars assuring the depositors that the bank was safe. But he was alarmed when he learned of the report of the national bank examiner made in January, 1874,[3] but which he had not seen before he became president. Nevertheless, he assured the public that the existing deficit could soon be made good. He further explained that the troubles had been caused by the forced sale of the bank's best securities during runs which had been brought about by newspaper criticisms.[4]

But his suspicions were soon aroused by the evident efforts of the actuary and others to keep

[2] Douglas Report, p. 31.

[3] See pp. 84, 151.

[4] Letter, dated April 29, to New York *Herald*, in Bruce Report, Appendix, p. 44. See below, pp. 151-156.

him in ignorance of what was going on. He found that confidential correspondence was carried on in a cipher to which he was not given a key. When he inquired about this he was made to understand that it was some one else's business. Sperry, however, who was one of the "reform" leaders, stated to the Bruce Committee that the cipher was used to prevent hostile newspapers from getting news of the condition of the bank; that telegraph operators would give information to reporters if telegrams were not in cipher code.[5]

THE COMPTROLLER'S REPORT

Without full knowledge of the real situation Douglass had continued to be somewhat hopeful until the publication of the full report of the Comptroller of the Currency. This report was based on the investigation made by a national bank examiner[6] and it showed that the Freedmen's Bank faced a large deficit, that it was loaded with poor securities, and that its business was practically at a standstill. Douglass was now convinced that the institution was beyond redemption. He had already discovered that it needed money badly.[7] One day Stickney, and Alvord the ex-president, who, it seems, hovered near to help run things, told Douglass that in order to prevent the bank from closing at once

[5] Bruce Report, pp. 237, 244, and Appendix, pp. 47–49.

[6] See p. 151.

[7] A report made on October 9, 1875, by the officer in charge of the accounts of the defunct Freedmen's Bureau indicates that the authorities of the Bureau had at times made loans of their funds to the bank. This action he thought was illegal and had resulted in the large deficits shown in the accounts of the Bureau. When the Bureau was discontinued, the bank missed the use of these large sums.—*Ho. Ex. Doc.* No. 144, 44 Cong., 1 Sess.

an immediate loan of $10,000 was necessary and that it could not be secured from outside sources. So they asked him for and secured a loan of $10,000 in United States bonds which he, Douglass, had on deposit. Douglass declared that it was with difficulty that he recovered the $10,000. When he discovered that the trustees and officials were withdrawing their deposits, he turned to Congress for relief.[8]

STATEMENT OF DOUGLASS

In his *Life and Times*, Douglass narrates his experience as president of the moribund bank. The account is so interesting and so well describes the situation that it is here reproduced:

It is not altogether without a feeling of humiliation that I must narrate my connection with the "Freedmen's Savings and Trust Company." This was an institution designed to furnish a place of security and profit for the hard earnings of the colored people, especially at the South. Though its title was the "Freedmen's Savings and Trust Company," it is known as the "Freedmen's Bank." According to its managers it was to be this and something more. There was something missionary in its composition, and it dealt largely in exhortations as well as promises. The men connected with its management were generally church members, and reputed eminent for their piety. Some of its agents had been preachers of the "Word." Their aim was now to instill into the minds of the untutored Africans lessons of sobriety, wisdom, and economy, and to show them how to rise in the world. Like snowflakes in winter, circulars, tracts and other papers were, by this benevolent institution, scattered among the sable millions, and they were told to "look" to the Freedmen's Bank and "live." Branches were established in all the

[8] Bruce Report, pp. 236, and Appendix, p. 44; *Ho. Misc. Doc.* No. 16, 43 Cong., 2 Sess.; New York *Herald*, May 1, 1874; Douglas Report, p. 178; Douglass, *Life and Times*, pp. 488–490.

southern states, and as a result, money to the amount of millions flowed into its vaults.

With the usual effect of sudden wealth, the managers felt like making a little display of their prosperity. They accordingly erected on one of the most desirable and expensive sites in the national capital, one of the most costly and splendid buildings of the time, finished on the inside with black walnut and furnished with marble counters and all modern improvements. The magnificent dimensions of the building bore testimony to its flourishing condition. In passing it on the street I often peeped into its spacious windows, and looked down the row of its gentlemanly and elegantly dressed colored clerks, with their pens behind their ears and button-hole bouquets in their coat-fronts, and felt my very eyes enriched. It was a sight I had never expected to see. I was amazed with the facility with which they counted the money. They threw off the thousands with the dexterity, if not the accuracy, of old experienced clerks. The whole thing was beautiful. I had read of this bank when I lived in Rochester, and had indeed been solicited to become one of its trustees, and had reluctantly consented to do so: but when I came to Washington and saw its magnificent brown stone front, its towering height, its perfect appointments and the fine display it made in the transaction of its business, I felt like the Queen of Sheba when she saw the riches of Solomon, that "the half had not been told me."

After settling myself down in Washington in the office of the *New Era*, I could and did occasionally attend the meetings of the Board of Trustees, and had the pleasure of listening to the rapid reports of the condition of the institution, which was generally of a most encouraging character. My confidence in the integrity and wisdom of the management was such that at one time I had entrusted to its vaults about twelve thousand. It seemed fitting to me to cast in my lot with my brother freedmen and to help build up an institution which represented their thrift and economy to so striking advantage; for the more millions accumulated there, I thought, the more consideration and respect would be shown to the colored people of the whole country.

About four months before this splendid institution was compelled to close its doors in the starved and deluded faces of its depositors, and while I was assured by its President and by its Actuary of its sound condition, I was solicited by some of its trustees to use my name in the board as a candidate for its presidency. So, I waked up one morning to find myself seated in a comfortable arm chair, with gold spectacles on my nose, and to hear myself addressed as President of the Freedmen's Bank. I could not help reflecting on the contrast between Frederick the slave boy, running about at Col. Lloyd's with only a tow linen shirt to cover him, and Frederick—President of a bank counting its assets by millions. I had heard of golden dreams, but such dreams had no comparison with this reality. And yet this seeming reality was scarcely more substantial than a dream. My term of service on this golden height covered only the brief space of three months, and these three months were divided into two parts, during the first part of which I was quietly employed in an effort to find out the real condition of the bank and its numerous branches. This was no easy task. On paper, and from the representations of its management, its assets amounted to three millions of dollars, and its liabilities were about equal to its assets. With such showing I was encouraged in the belief that by curtailing the expenses, and doing away with the non-paying branches, which policy the trustees had now adopted, we could be carried safely through the financial distress then upon the country.

So confident was I of this, that in order to meet what was said to be a temporary emergency, I was induced to loan the bank ten thousand dollars of my money, to be held by it until it could realize on a part of its abundant securities. This money, though it was repaid, was not done so as promptly as, under the supposed circumstances, I thought it should be, and these circumstances increased my fears lest the chasm was not so easily bridged as the actuary of the institution had assured me it could be. The more I observed and learned the more my confidence diminished. I found that those trustees who wished to issue cards and publish addresses professing the utmost confidence in the bank, had themselves not one dollar deposited there. Some of them, while strongly assuring me of its soundness had withdrawn their money and opened accounts elsewhere.

Gradually I discovered that the bank had, through dishonest agents, sustained heavy losses at the South; that there was a discrepancy on the books of forty thousand dollars for which no account could be given, and that, instead of our assets being equal to our liabilities, we could not in all likelihoods of the case pay seventy-two cents on the dollar. There was an air of mystery, too, about the spacious and elegant apartments of the bank building, which greatly troubled me, and which I have only been able to explain to myself on the supposition that the employees, from the actuary and the inspector down to the messengers, were (perhaps) naturally anxious to hold their places, and consequently have the business continued. I am not a violent advocate of the doctrine of total depravity of human nature. I am inclined, on the whole, to believe it a tolerable good nature, yet instances do occur which oblige me to concede that men can and do act from mere personal and selfish motives. In this case, at any rate, it seemed not unreasonable to conclude that the finely dressed young gentlemen, adorned with pens and bouquets, the most fashionable and genteel of all our colored youth, stationed behind those marble counters, should desire to retain their places as long as there was money in the vaults to pay them their salaries.

Standing on the platform of this large and complicated establishment, with its thirty-four branches, extending from New Orleans to Philadelphia, its machinery in full operation, its correspondence carried on in cipher, its actuary dashing in and out of the bank with an air of pressing business, if not of bewilderment, I found the path of enquiry I was pursuing an exceedingly difficult one. I knew there had been very lately several runs on the bank, and that there had been a heavy draft made upon its reserve fund, but I did not know, what I should have been told before being allowed to enter upon the duties of my office, that this reserve, which the bank by its charter was required to keep, had been entirely exhausted, and that hence there was nothing left to meet any future emergency.

Not to make too long a story, I was, in six weeks after my election as president of this bank, convinced that it was no longer a safe custodian of the hard earnings of my confiding people. This conclusion once reached, I could not hesitate as to my duty in the premises, and this was, to save as much as possible of the assets held by the bank for the benefit of the depositors; and to prevent their being further squandered in keeping up appearances, and in paying the salaries of myself and other officers in the bank. Fortunately, Congress, from which we held our charter, was then in session, and its committees on finance were in daily session. I felt it my duty to make known as speedily as possible to Hon. John Sherman, Chairman of the Senate Committee on Finance, and to Senator Scott of Pennsylvania, also of the same committee, that I regarded the institution as insolvent and irrecoverable, and that I could no longer ask my people to deposit money in it. This representation to the finance committee subjected me to very bitter opposition on the part of the officers of the bank. Its actuary, Mr. Stickney, immediately summoned some of its trustees, a dozen or so of them, to go before the [Senate] finance committee and make a counter statement to that made by me; and this they did. Some of them who had assisted me by giving me facts showing the insolvency of the bank, now made haste to contradict that conclusion and to assure the committee that it was, if allowed to go on, abundantly able to weather the financial storm and pay dollar for dollar to its depositors.

I was not exactly thunderstruck, but I was much amazed by the contradiction. I, however, adhered to my statement that the bank ought to stop. The finance committee substantially agreed with me and in a few weeks so legislated, by appointing three commissioners to take charge of its affairs, as to bring this imposing banking business to a close.

This is a fair and unvarnished narration of my connection with the Freedmen's Savings and Trust Company, otherwise known as the Freedmen's Savings Bank, a connection which has brought upon my head an amount of abuse and detraction greater than any encountered in any other part of my life.

Before leaving the subject I ought in justice to myself to state that, when I found that the affairs of the bank were to be closed up, I did not, as I might easily have done, and as others did, make myself a preferred creditor and take my money out of the bank, but on the contrary, I determined to take my chances with the other depositors, and left my money, to the amount of two thousand dollars, to be divided with the assets among the creditors of the bank. And now, after seven years have been allowed for the value of the securities to appreciate and the loss of interest on the deposits for that length of time, the depositors may deem themselves fortunate if they receive sixty cents on the dollar of what they placed in the care of the fine savings institution.

It is also due to myself to state, especially since I have seen myself accused of bringing the Freedmen's Bank into ruin, and squandering in senseless loans on bad security the hardly-earned moneys of my race, that all the loans ever made by the bank were made prior to my connection with it as its president. Not a dollar, not a dime of its millions were loaned by me, or with my approval. The fact is, and all investigation shows it, that I was married to a corpse. The false building, with its marble counters and black walnut finishings, was there, as were the affable and agile clerks and the discreet and colored cashier; but the Life, which was the money, was gone, and I found that I had been placed there with the hope that by "some drugs, some charms, some conjuration, or some mighty magic," I would bring it back.[9]

CONGRESS INTERVENES

So, as he has related, Douglass, believing that the interests of the depositors could be protected only by Congress, insisted to the Senate Committee on Finance that immediate action by Congress was necessary. He told the Bruce

[9] Douglass, *Life and Times*, pp. 487-493.

Committee in 1876: "I began to discredit the bank in the eyes of the Banking Committee of the Senate. . . . I spent my time mostly in doing that sort of business."[10]

As a result Douglass with the aid of the Senate Committee secured the passage of an act[11] which in effect placed the bank in liquidation and authorized the establishment of a new bank which should have the same name. There was much sentiment in favor of continuing the Freedmen's Bank and some interested parties believed that in a new organization the mistakes which had ruined the old one might be avoided.

THE BANK TO BE REORGANIZED

The principal provisions of this new law were as follows: The business of the past was to be separated from that of the future; loans made outside of the state in which the money was collected were to be called in; non-paying branches were to be closed with the consent of the Secretary of the Treasury, and all their accounts settled. The new administration was to invest one-half of all deposits in United States securities, or keep them on deposit in a national bank; it was authorized to make loans out of the remainder of the deposits on real estate not only in the District of Columbia, but also in the vicinity of the branches. The rate of interest paid on deposits was limited to five per cent; no loan over $10,000 could be made to one person and the security must be double the value of the

[10] Bruce Report, p. 237; Douglass, *Life and Times*, p. 491.
[11] Approved June 20, 1874, see Appendix, p. 136.

loan. Deposits made after the date of this law
(June 20, 1874) were to be considered "special"
and held for the use of the depositor. But if, after
the report which was to be made by the trustees
on the condition of the bank, the Secretary of the
Treasury should pronounce the concern solvent,
then these last deposits might be turned into the
general fund and the business go on as before.

The above provisions were meant in part to
save appearances and to afford the trustees an
opportunity to get out of their difficulties if it
were possible. But as it resulted the real sig-
nificance of the act was in the section which
provided that, if the trustees thought it proper,
they might nominate three commissioners to be
appointed by the Secretary of the Treasury to
close up the bank and its branches, collect its
loans, realize on its investments, and pay the
proceeds to the depositors.[12]

After the passage of this act there was a faint
pretense at reorganization. The trustees lowered
the interest rate on deposits to five per cent, decreased the number of employees and prepared
to discontinue some of the non-paying branches.
Douglass himself seems to have been optimistic
for he issued a circular stating that the bank was
now on a firm basis and that the $217,000 deficit
could be diminished under careful management.
The trouble had been caused, he said, by non-
paying branches, too high interest rate, "senseless runs," hostility to the Negro race and hence
to the Negro bank, and general hard times.

[12] Bruce Report, pp. 238, 239 and Appendix; Douglass, *Life and
Times*, p. 491.

There had been, he stated, too much competition with old and well established banks and too rapid expansion which had resulted in too many weak paying branches. Promising economy and prudence in future management, he showed that new depositors were protected from old debts of the institution, while the best arrangement possible had been made for the old depositors. Hereafter, he stated, the constant drain of deposits to Washington from all over the country would cease, and investments would be made in the vicinity of the branches. This last concession, he explained, was in response to a widespread objection on the part of the depositors to the practice of sending in all deposits to Washington or New York.[13]

The trustees tried to begin reform by making Stickney, the actuary, give bond as required by law. It was found that he had held his position for two years and had never made bond. At first, it seems, he had not been asked to make bond, and later, when requested to do so, he refused on the ground that the business of the bank was so involved that it was not safe for him to comply. Now when called before the trustees, who suspected him of crooked practices, he again refused to give bond, and as Purvis, one of the trustees, said: "Then Stickney commenced to cry. That was pretty good evidence of his guilt for we were not in a prayer meeting."[14]

[13] Bruce Report, Appendix. For example, Rainey, a Negro congressman from South Carolina, complained that the South Carolina Negroes had put half a million in the bank but that not a dollar had been loaned in the state.—*Cong. Record*, March 3, 1875, p. 2262.

[14] Bruce Report, p. 139, and the report of the committee; Douglas Report, p. 76.

THE BANK IS CLOSED

In a few days it was found that the bank as a business institution was dead. The trustees decided on June 28, 1874, to close the doors and to nominate commissioners to wind up affairs. But even the last days were not free from queer practices on the part of the officers. On June 30, 1874, the day after closing, we find that one Juan Boyle borrowed from Stickney on slender security, $33,366.66. Stickney later explained this by saying that Boyle had the money already but that the bank had no evidence of the debt. Consequently on June 30 he had accepted Boyle's note and any security that the latter was willing to give. This, he thought, was better than nothing. Later the commissioners found that Boyle had been employed by Alvord to sell securities for the bank and that out of each transaction he had kept back money until he was due the bank $33,366.66. But this matter like several others was never fully cleared up.[15]

Stickney and the bookkeepers also violated the law of June 20, 1874, by not keeping all deposits made after the passage of the law separate from the business of earlier date.[16] And, further, after the bank was closed Stickney withdrew the Rost Home Colony fund[17] and carried it to a new bank—"The People's Bank"—organized by himself.[18]

[15] Bruce Report, pp. 140, 157, 181.

[16] Bruce Report, p. 15.

[17] See above, p. 34.

[18] Douglas Report, pp. 77, 78, 182, 187.

CONDITION OF THE BANK IN 1874

As nearly as can be ascertained there was due to depositors at the date of closing the sum of $2,993,790.68 on 61,144 accounts. In the vaults was found only $400 in United States securities and in the branches cash amounting to $31,689.35 —all the rest had gone out in personal and real estate loans which could be realized upon only with difficulty and after long delay. The worst loans had been made from the "available" fund and here the heaviest losses finally fell. The most troublesome loans were divided as follows:

From the "available" fund......$2,175,174.99 to 146 persons
From other funds.............. 585,333.19 to 154 persons

The latest statement that can be obtained from the branches is that of January 24, 1874, which is given below. It will show approximately how the deposits and therefore the losses were distributed.[19]

AMOUNT OF DEPOSITS AT THE BRANCHES, JANUARY 24, 1874

Branches	Deposits	Branches	Deposits
Alexandria, Va.	$ 21,584	Little Rock, Ark........	$ 17,728
Atlanta, Ga.............	28,404	Louisville, Ky.........	137,094
Augusta, Ga...........	96,882	Lynchburg, Va.........	19,967
Baltimore, Md..........	303,947	Macon, Ga...:........	54,342
Beaufort, S. C.........	55,592	Memphis, Tenn........	96,755
Charleston, S. C.......	255,345	Mobile, Ala.	95,144
Columbus, Miss.	18,857	Montgomery, Ala.......	29,743
Columbia, Tenn.........	19,823	Natchez, Miss.	22,195
Huntsville, Ala.	35,963	Nashville, Tenn........	78,525
Jacksonville, Fla.......	22,022	New Bern, N. C........	40,621
Lexington, Ky.........	34,193	New Orleans, La.......	240,006

Bruce Report, pp. 299–307 and Appendix, p. 22. *Ho. Misc. Doc.* No. 16, 43 Cong., 2 Sess.

[19] *Ho. Misc. Doc.* 16, 43 Cong., 2 Sess., p. 61. Meigs Report, Feb. 24, 1874; *Bankers' Magazine*, June, 1875; July, 1881; *The Nation*, April 15, 1875.

New York, N. Y.	344,071	Saint Louis, Mo.	58,397
Norfolk, Va.	126,337	Tallahassee, Fla.	40,207
Philadelphia, Pa.	84,657	Vicksburg, Miss.	114,348
Raleigh, N. C.	26,703	Washington, D. C.	384,789
Richmond, Va.	166,000	Wilmington, N. C.	45,223
Savannah, Ga.	153,425		
Shreveport, La.	30,312	Total	$3,299,201

Thus ended in failure a most promising plan to aid the Negro race. The various causes leading to this failure have been discussed at length and may be summed up as follows: Poor business management; neglect of duty by the more honest and capable trustees; the failure of Congress to make an investigation in time; the general depression of business in 1873; hostility to the bank as a race institution and as a connection of the Freedmen's Bureau; dishonesty and incompetency in the branches; and finally and fundamentally the careless and corrupt use of its funds by the "ring" of District of Columbia trustees and officials.

The Freedmen's Bank had a fine field and according to expert opinion could have survived all other troubles had it not been for the lack of honesty on the part of those who for a time controlled its management at Washington. Like so many other enterprises throughout the United States during that period it fell a prey to the general corruption that prevailed during the Reconstruction period.[20]

[20] Bruce Report, pp. 248, 249, 273, 274; Douglas Report, p. 17; *Cong. Record* April 22 (1876), p. 2707. See Oberholtzer, *Jay Cooke*, *passim*, as to banking conditions in the 1870's.

Chapter VII

THE WORK OF THE COMMISSIONERS

THE COMMISSIONERS

THERE was a struggle among the members of the board of trustees over the nomination of the three commissioners provided for in the law of June 20, 1874. Douglass, whose efforts had secured the legislation that resulted in the closing of the bank, insisted that the commissioners should have no connection with the trustees. Those who ruined the bank, he said, ought to have nothing to do with winding up its affairs. But by the act referred to, the trustees were authorized to nominate the commissioners, and forthwith three relatives of trustees were named—just what Douglass had feared.[1] However, the Secretary of the Treasury refused to appoint them, and these new nominations were then made: John A. J. Creswell, formerly Postmaster General; R. H. T. Leipold, a Treasury accountant, said to be related to John Sherman; and Robert Purvis,[2] a Philadel-

[1] Bruce Report, p. 239.

[2] Robert Purvis, born 1810, Charleston, S. C., was the son of a white father and a "Moorish" mother. Going North he attained some prominence as an anti-slavery worker. His son Charles B. Purvis, a physician, was later surgeon-in-chief of the Freedmen's Hospital in the District of Columbia and Professor in the Medical Department of Howard University. In describing conditions in South Carolina during Reconstruction J. M. Morgan in *Recollections of a Rebel Reefer*, p. 329, makes this

101

phia Negro, the father of Dr. Purvis, the Negro
trustee. These men were then appointed by the
Secretary of the Treasury. Leipold was chosen
by the trustees because he was an expert accountant; Creswell, "because he was a cabinet
officer, the most practical Republican we ever
had," and because he had a reputation for appointing Negroes to office;[3] Purvis was chosen
because of his color, a Negro being needed to
represent the race.

The commissioners took charge of the affairs
of the defunct bank on July 11, 1874. The salary
of each was fixed at $3,000 a year and they were
required by the Secretary of the Treasury to
make a joint bond for $100,000. From the first
there was trouble among them in regard to the
proper division of the work and responsibilities.
Creswell and Purvis did practically nothing but
sign the checks for dividends (quite a task, however) and they soon made it evident that they
did not intend to undertake other duties, but to
leave the business for Leipold to look after.
Creswell seemed to think that his part was done
by allowing the use of his name and his reputation as a friend of the Negroes; and Purvis
seemed to feel that his part was merely to be a
Negro member on the board of commissioners.

statement: "Cardozo, a Negro, was superintendent of Public Education
and Purvis, a Philadelphia mulatto, was Adjutant General of the state.
These two men were considered by the natives to be the most respectable
members of the state government." Possibly this Purvis was one of
those connected with the Freedmen's Savings Bank.

[3] Creswell was a native of Maryland, and in politics had been a
Whig, later a Democrat, and finally a Radical Republican. He served as
congressman and senator from Maryland during the Civil War, and in
1869 he became Postmaster General, resigning on July 3, 1874.

Leipold, an exceedingly unpleasant though very efficient person, was soon at loggerheads with the other commissioners because they would not work, and for other personal reasons.

DISAGREEMENTS AMONG THE COMMISSIONERS

Purvis drew his salary to the last for being a Negro member, and Creswell drew his for being a friend of the Negroes. Leipold, who was certainly not a friend of the Negroes, treated rudely all of them who had business with the commissioners. Purvis, who had all the American Negro's dislike of foreigners, complained that Leipold was a lowborn, bad-mannered, foreign fortune hunter, whose eccentricities amounted almost to craziness, but both Purvis and Creswell testified that their disagreeable colleague was an efficient business man.[4]

The squabbles among the commissioners soon attracted the attention of the public. Some were as interesting and about as dignified as a dog fight. Leipold objected to being made the only burden bearer, but when he suggested that the other members do some of the work or pay for assistants to do it, the latter were quite indignant. Creswell recalled that when he was nominated the trustees told him: "General, we don't want your time, we want your name." "Mr. Leipold," Creswell said, "was to have charge of the details and Mr. Purvis and myself were to assist in all matters of advice and generally in the conduct of affairs." When Leipold complained later that he had been "the pack horse

[4] Bruce Report, pp. 73–89, 127, 128, 187, 239, and report of the committee; Douglas Report, p. 77.

of the concern," Creswell asserted that he himself was in the bank "one whole month" and "every summer for three or four years in order to supervise." "Mr. Leipold," he conceded, "is a very competent accountant. I believe that he has faithfully and rigidly looked after the interests of the depositors, but he is the most disagreeable person with whom I have ever associated. His temper and manners are exceedingly disagreeable and at times almost insupportable."[5]

Purvis stated that he and Creswell were not expected to work but to "contribute our eminent respectability," yet he had spent as much as ten days at the bank. "I came here," he said, "to represent the colored people whose confidence I have." "I was there to watch him [Leipold]. I will say that the colored people, the depositors, looked mainly to me, for they had confidence in me, to see that it was properly done, and they used frequently to say to me, 'If it were not for you we would not get a dollar.' " As for Leipold, Purvis said that he, in making such "a sneaking assault"[6] was "guilty of an act of perfidy so treacherous that there is no parallel in the scope of my experience of bad men and bad acts." He had paid Leipold $500, "purely as a benefaction," he said, on account of his "snivelling whining about his poverty." But he added: "There was, however, a faithfulness in the discharge of his duties." Purvis also objected to Leipold's smoking and put up a sign: "Gentlemen will not smoke in this room," claiming, he

[5] Bruce Report, pp. 80, 81.

[6] That is, in complaining that Purvis and Creswell were doing no work.

said, "equal rights." Leipold then suggested that
"equal rights and equal duties" go together.
Creswell persuaded Purvis to take uown his
sign.[7]

There were other causes of the lack of harmony
among these officials. As Leipold was regarded
by the Treasury Department as the most competent and responsible commissioner, he received
advice from the Secretary of the Treasury in
regard to the business. Both Secretary Sherman
and his successor, Secretary Boutwell, disliked
Creswell and held Purvis in slight regard. Purvis
and Creswell resented this attitude of the Treasury officials and vented their outraged feelings
upon Leipold. When law work was needed Purvis wanted to employ Negro lawyers, but Leipold
would have none of them. Leipold suspected
crookedness among the former trustees and collected information upon which to base prosecutions against some of them, among them Purvis'
son who had been interested in loans made by
the bank. Creswell advised against prosecutions,
and Purvis, a warm partisan of the trustees,
stoutly defended all their activities. He accused
Leipold of "ingratitude" because he wanted to
prosecute those who had nominated him as commissioner. Leipold met such strong opposition
from his colleagues that he found it impossible
to prosecute any of the trustees even for such
doings as the Seneca Sandstone deal.[8]

THE INFLUENCE OF THE TRUSTEES

The trustees of the defunct bank continued to

[7] Bruce Report, pp. 62, 74.
[8] Bruce Report, pp. 91–95.

maintain some kind of an organization and were several times called together by Dr. Purvis (son of Commissioner Purvis) to consider the actions of the commissioners and to give them advice and instructions. Creswell and Purvis who seemed to think that the trustees had a right to advise, gave considerable attention to their wishes, but Leipold took the view that the board of trustees no longer existed and refused to permit any interference. This stand greatly angered the Purvises.[9]

Several attempts, probably inspired by Leipold, were made to get measures through Congress directing the commissioners to bring suit against trustees, officials, and agents who were charged with illegal practices. These efforts though supported, it was rumored, by the Treasury Department, were opposed by the friends of the trustees and by the Negro members of Congress, and resulted each time in failure.[10]

OPPOSITION TO THE COMMISSIONERS

Among those interested in the bank, there was some hostility to each individual commissioner and much unfavorable criticism of them collectively on account of their disagreements and their methods of work. So unpleasant was their position and their personal relations that all would have resigned in a body, but they were informed by the Attorney General that only by an act of Congress could they be relieved of their

[9] Bruce Report, pp. 62, 74, 78.

[10] *Congressional Globe*, March 3, 1875, p. 2262, and Dec. 14, 1875, p. 207; *Bankers' Magazine*, June, 1875.

duties and released from their joint bond of $100,000. Between 1875 and 1881 several bills were introduced into Congress to abolish the board of commissioners and turn the business over to one man. Among those who introduced such bills were Senator Sherman and Representatives Douglas of Virginia and Durham of Kentucky.[11] The object of the bills was to legislate Purvis and Creswell out of office and leave Leipold to wind up the business as rapidly as possible. Durham proposed that Congress provide for the purchase of the Freedmen's Bank building,[12] order the prosecution of the trustees against whom evidence of fraud existed, and replace the three commissioners, whose powers were inadequate, with one man (presumably Leipold) empowered to close up the business at once under the supervision of the Secretary of Treasury. The friends of Creswell, Purvis, and the trustees united in opposition to this and other measures and succeeded in defeating them. Rainey, a Negro congressman from South Carolina, was the chief advocate of Purvis and Creswell.[13]

[11] Durham's bill was strongly opposed by General B. F. Butler of Massachusetts and by Randall of Pennsylvania, both of whom wanted to prevent Purvis of Philadelphia from being legislated out of office. Randall said that since the whites had done so badly by the Negroes the latter would have confidence only in a board which contained a colored man. Senator Hawley of Connecticut opposed the Durham bill because he did not think that the bank affairs should be settled by the Secretary of the Treasury but ought to be handled as usual through bankruptcy proceedings.—*Cong. Record*, January 26, 1875, pp. 751, 752 and March 3, 1875, p. 2261.

[12] This building was leased in 1874 to the government for the use of the Attorney General at a rental of $14,000 a year. Finally it was purchased by the government and occupied by the Court of Claims.—Bruce Report, p. 21.

[13] *Bankers' Magazine*, June, 1875.

INVESTIGATIONS BY CONGRESS

While the commissioners were wrangling, and the friends of the Negroes were trying to induce Congress to settle the affairs of the bank, two congressional investigations into the affairs of the institution were made—one in 1876 by the Douglas Committee, and another in 1880 by the Bruce Committee. Both investigations were made at the instance of the southern Democrats and the Negro Republican members from the southern states. Most of the northern members of Congress objected to the waste of any more time and trouble on the Freedmen's Bank. Both political factions in the South were willing to throw responsibility for the mismanagement of the bank upon individuals affiliated with the northern Republicans.[14]

These investigations laid bare the fraudulent methods and corrupt practices by which the bank had been brought to' ruin. The report of the Douglas Committee, after giving a historical sketch of the bank, went into details in regard to the causes of its failure, asserting that some of the trustees were honorable men, but that the controlling members, especially after the removal of headquarters to Washington, were either sharpers or dupes; that the law failed to make the trustees liable to penalties for misuse of the funds under their control; that there was no

[14] The Douglas Committee from the House consisted of Douglas of Virginia, chairman; Bradford, of Alabama; Stenger, of Pennsylvania; Riddle, of Tennessee; Hooker and Bliss, of New York; Frost, of Massachusetts; and Rainey (Negro) of South Carolina. The Bruce Committee from the Senate was composed of B. K. Bruce (Negro) of Mississippi, chairman; Angus Cameron of Wisconsin; John B. Gordon of Georgia; Robert E. Withers of Virginia; and A. H. Garland of Arkansas.

warrant in law for the establishment of the branch banks; that the inspection was of little or no value because there was no disposition on the part of the authorities to remedy the defects reported by the inspectors; that the passage of the Act of 1870 was secured by and for the interest of the "Washington cabal" and the downfall of the bank was thereby hastened. After condemning in detail the doings of the District of Columbia interests the committee recommended that the work of the three commissioners be turned over to one man in order to reduce the expenses of administration.[15] The concluding section of the report, quite Democratic in tone, is as follows:

The inspectors provided by the by-laws were of little or no value, either through the connivance and ignorance of the inspectors or the indifference of the trustees to their reports. . . . The committee of examination . . . were still more careless and inefficient, while the board of trustees, as a supervising and administrative body, intrusted with the fullest power of general control over the management, proved utterly faithless to the trust reposed in them. Everything was left to the actuary and finance committee. Such was the practical working of the machine. . . . The depositors were of small account compared with the personal interest of the political jobbers, real estate pools, and fancy stock speculators, who were organizing a raid upon the freedmen's money and resorted to an amendment of the charter to facilitate their operations.

The District of Columbia government, too, came in to hasten and profit by the work of spoliation thus inaugu-

[15] The Douglas Report is *House Report*, No. 502, 44 Cong., 2 Sess. It contains thirteen pages of the committee report and 241 pages of testimony, documents, records of branch banks, tables of statistics and statements of the commissioners. Thirty officials and depositors testified before the committee.

rated. Its treasury was wholly unequal to the task of sustaining the magnificent expenditures of the board of public works, presided over by H. D. Cooke, and controlled by Mr. A. R. Shepherd. Some exchequer must be found to advance upon the depreciated bonds and worthless auditor's certificates of the District, or the contracts must fail, and the speculators of the pool and of Shepherd and his friends in out-of-the-way and unimproved town lots come to grief. This mass of putridity, the District government, now abhorred of all men, and abandoned and repudiated even by the political authors of its being, was represented in the bank by no less than five of its high officers, viz., H. D. Cooke, George W. Balloch, William S. Huntington, D. L. Eaton, and Z. B. Richards, all of whom were in one way or other concerned in speculations more or less dependent for a successful issue on sustaining the contractors under the board of public works, and a free use of the funds of the Freedmen's Bank. They were high in power, too, with the dominant influence in Congress, as the legislation they asked or sanctioned and obtained, fully demonstrated.

Thus it was that without consulting the wishes or regarding the interests of those most concerned—the depositors—the vaults of the bank were literally thrown open to unscrupulous greed and rapacity. The toilsome savings of the poor Negroes, hoarded and laid by for a rainy day, through the carelessness and dishonest connivance of their self-constituted guardians, melted away—vanished into thin air in the form of millions of so-called assets, on which by no possible contingency can fifty cents on the dollar be ever realized to the unfortunate victims of heartless duplicity and misplaced confidence. The wolves literally became the pastors of the flock, and, without compunction or remorse, devoured the younglings committed to their care.

In the foregoing narrative your committee have necessarily, though somewhat incidentally, touched upon and pointed out the prime, but remote and indirect, causes of failure of the Freedmen's Bank—which was the utter and complete omission to provide in the law of its organization any safeguards for the protection of the depositors, who were encouraged and invited to trust their millions to its keeping. . . .

And now, taking a retrospective glance over the events of the last ten years, in which this Freedmen's Bank looms up conspicuously, we are led to believe that no race or kindred among all the generations of men have so thoroughly sounded the depths of the philosophy expressed in the prayer, "save me from my friends," as those "persons lately held in slavery" at the South, a people over whom more crocodile tears have been shed, on whom more imposition practiced, and for whom less real sympathy felt by their professed friends, than any other known to history—a people almost literally stabbed under the fifth rib with a hug and a salutation, "How is it with thee today, my brother?" In regard to this bank, the grossest deception was practiced upon them. They were told that it was a Government institution, and its solvency and safety guaranteed by the United States. Missionaries, of whom the chief was Alvord, perambulated the South mixing religion, politics, education, and teaching the blacks how "to toil and to save," and then trust their hard earned savings to Alvord and his associates to invest them, not until, however, they had levied toll for their services in bestowing such inestimable benefits, and for their disinterested labors and sacrifices.

Full of gratitude to the Government for his emancipation, the Negro was easily approached by and gave unheeding to any adventurer who declared himself his friend and professed a desire to aid his moral, intellectual, and social elevation, provided he belonged to the party of the administration. He believed and was deceived, trusted and was betrayed. Taught, to his ruin and that of the whites among whom he lives and moves and has his being, and between whom and himself there must be mutual trust and confidence before prosperity can be restored to his section, to hate and distrust the "old master classes," he is now derided by his old friends for credulity . . . and told that those who dragged him out of slavery have by that one act cancelled every obligation to deal with him on principles of common honesty.

Upon no one of the originators and trustees of the bank did so great responsibility rest as upon John W. Alvord, but yet he permitted all the misdoings described in this report to go on from year to year without any vigorous protest or effort to correct them, and, so far from giving warnings to those who had so trusted the concern through his persuasion, he helped to keep up the delusion by praising it, enlarging upon its benefits, giving assurances of its stability and soliciting increase of depositors and deposits.

The Bruce Committee which reported on April 2, 1880, went over much of the same ground and arrived at similar conclusions. Additional evidence was found in regard to the negligence and misconduct of the trustees and more details about doubtful loans were brought out. The committee declared that the administration of the three commissioners was too expensive, and it recommended that all the business be turned over to the Comptroller of the Currency, a recommendation which was followed a year later.[16]

The debate that followed the introduction of each measure aimed at settling the affairs of the bank showed that the members of Congress felt that they as a body were partly responsible for the failure of the bank. Bradford, of Alabama, stating that the government was to some extent responsible for the Negro's faith in the bank maintained that Congress ought not to shirk its duty to the depositors. He also asserted that the corrupt administration of the bank was only a

[16] The report of this committee is *Senate Report*, No. 440, 46 Cong., 2 Sess. It contains eleven pages of committee report, 319 pages of testimony by 21 witnesses, and 17 pages of documents. The reports of the Douglas and the Bruce committees are the best sources of information in regard to the Freedmen's Savings Bank.

phase of the general misgovernment all over the
South after 1868, that it was a logical outcome
of the policy of the administration at Washington, and he further showed that the bank officials
were closely connected with the administration.
Naturally this way of proving the responsibility
of Congress did not appeal to the Republicans.

Bradford further declared that "since the government was organized no such stupendous fraud
has ever existed under its protection." It was not
meant, he said, that there should be any branch
banks, but the speculators wanted them for the
purpose of draining the money from the South.
They "went as missionaries all over the land and
declared to the colored people of the southern
country that this bank would take care of this
fund for them and that its management and its
solvency were guaranteed by the United States
government." Weak officials were chosen in
order that others might use them as tools, and
the bank had been treated as the carpetbaggers
and the Federal administration had treated the
entire country.[17]

Other southern congressmen seized the opportunity to score the "friends of the Negro." When
in 1875 Durham of Kentucky was trying to have
an act passed to relieve the depositors, he was
opposed by such Republicans as Hawley of Connecticut, who objected, on the ground of "sympathy for the Negro," to any measure that would
legislate Purvis, the Negro commissioner, out of
office. Durham answered him thus: "These

[17] See Bradford's speech in *Cong. Record*, April 22, 1876, pp. 2701–
2708.

72,000 depositors . . . do not care very much about sympathy provided only they get their money. They have been sympathized with by their friends until they have been literally robbed. These friends of the colored people have hugged them around the neck with one hand while they have stolen the money out of their pockets with the other."[18]

Some of the northern members acknowledged a certain responsibility on the part of Congress for the condition of the bank. Senator Morrill admitted that Congress was largely responsible, for, as he said, "we certainly gave this institution of the Freedmen's Bank some sort of credit throughout the country." He thought the original trustees should have been prosecuted.[19] Senator Cameron, of Pennsylvania, contented himself with reminding the Senate that he had predicted the failure of the bank as a result of the amendment of 1870.[20] Senator Sherman, who had persistently tried to induce Congress to regulate the bank, declared that "the original management of the Freedmen's Bank grossly and scandalously abused its trust; and all the powers conferred by Congress on that corporation were in my judgment abused."[21]

THE TASK OF THE COMMISSIONERS

But until 1881 all the debates concerning the bank resulted in no action, and the commis-

[18] *Cong. Record*, March 3, 1875, p. 2262.
[19] *Cong. Record*, December 8, 1878, p. 36.
[20] See above, p. 72.
[21] *Cong. Record*, Feb. 5, 1877, pp. 1273, 1274.

sioners, failing to get relief from Congress, were
forced to proceed with their disagreeable task.
This task was to close up the branch banks and
transfer all accounts to Washington; to bring the
chaotic accounts of the institution into some
order; to manage the property belonging to it;
to collect debts and claims, to turn assets into
cash; and finally to pay dividends to the depositors as soon as funds were available. The Negroes were so averse to seeing the branches closed
that for several years it was necessary for the
commissioners to keep agents on small salaries[22]
at some of the old branches to explain the situation to the depositors and persuade them to send
in their claims.

Although the commissioners advertised far
and wide for the pass books to be turned in, the
depositors for a while held back, as their suspicions had been excited by that faction of the
trustees who had opposed the closing of the bank
and by the speculators who wanted to buy pass
books for a small fraction of their value. The
accounts of about 50,000 depositors were quite
small, and it was found that these were easily
discouraged and soon became somewhat indiffer-
ent. Some of the former trustees continued to
announce that the bank would certainly be re-
opened, declaring that the recent legislation of
Congress relating to the bank was merely a
Democratic attack upon the Negro race and that
the closing of the institution was nothing but a
political measure. Charges were also made that
Leipold was speculating in bank books. To pro-

[22] $10 to $25 a month.

tect depositors the commissioners ruled that no assignments would be allowed, and the pass books began to flow in.[23]

METHODS EMPLOYED BY THE COMMISSIONERS

When all of the accounts of the branch banks that could be obtained were collected in Washington, it was found impossible to reduce them to good order. Many Freedmen's Bureau accounts were turned in from the branch banks and papers belonging to the Freedmen's Bank were found in the Bureau archives. There was a difference of $42,297.50 between the accounts of the branches and the accounts at headquarters as to the balance due depositors. Pass books were found to be more nearly correct than the ledgers, so the depositors were paid according to their pass books. Each loan had to be investigated to see how much had been repaid and how much was still due. Seldom could a loan be collected without a lawsuit. Between 1874 and 1879 over three hundred cases were carried to court by the commissioners, but frequently the lawyers' fees took all, or nearly all, of the collections.

Every obstacle was put in the way of the commissioners. There was strong opposition by depositors in some localities to the sending to Washington of the proceeds of collections, as they believed that the money would never be returned. The courts in the different states and in the District of Columbia were easily prevailed upon to issue injunctions preventing the sale of property for the bank. Much property belonging

[23] Report of Commissioners, Dec. 14, 1874, in *Ho. Misc. Doc.*, No. 16, 43 Cong., 2 Sess.; Bruce Report, p. 17, and Appendix, p. 6.

to the branches was found to be almost without value.[24]

But the commissioners worked on, closing the branches one by one until only those in Nashville and Beaufort were left open. In order to avoid heavy losses the commissioners were obliged after foreclosure to buy in nearly all good property. And then owing to the depressed financial condition of the country, they frequently had to hold this property for years before it could be disposed of without loss. Meanwhile, much of the income from it was absorbed by the expenses of caretaking. The headquarters building in Washington was leased for a time for the use of the Attorney General and the Court of Claims and in 1882 was sold to the United States government for $250,000.[25]

Although at first the trustees tried to control or embarrass the policy of the commissioners, their efforts could be ignored, and their organization finally went to pieces. Creswell and Purvis were on friendly terms with them, but Leipold, advised by the Treasury Department, refused to allow them to have anything to do with the affairs of the bank. They took revenge by making charges against him of improper conduct in the administration of the business. Leipold was intensely disliked by the Negroes, who said that he "did not treat us politely, but would

[24] In Congress, Representative Small, a Negro, from South Carolina complained that the commissioners were acting in collusion with purchasers in South Carolina in selling property at low prices. The commissioners answered that it was difficult to sell property in the South at any price.—Bruce Report, p. 29; Reports of Commissioners, 1874–1879; Bruce Report, pp. 13, 17, 19, 31.

[25] Bruce Report, p. 38.

go on writing when we would speak to him."
He wanted to do some of the work himself for
the attorney's fees and remarked that he was
"not here to make sacrifices for the colored
race."[26] When the depositors would worry him
with questions he would say, "What are you
pestering me for?" He told them that they had
no business trusting such a bank—"Who ever
knew of a Freedmen's Bank? . . . If I had not
taken up this bank you would not have a dollar.
We brought you out of slavery. You had nothing
then and you need not think of these little
losses."[27] He was accused by his enemies of speculating in the property under his control and of
trying to purchase claims of depositors, but no
proof was ever adduced, and there is little likelihood of his having done so. Although he did not
like Negroes, he nevertheless managed their accounts with honesty and efficiency.[28]

DIVIDENDS

As money was collected by the commissioners
from loans and from sales it was placed in the
United States Treasury to await division among
the depositors. Although large sums were kept
in the Treasury, no interest was allowed by Congress, nor were the commissioners permitted to
invest the funds in interest-bearing United States
securities. Had this been done the income would
have gone far to cover the rather heavy expenses
of administration. On December 2, 1878, the
three commissioners united in a letter to Speaker

[26] Douglas Report, pp. 77, 165, 166.
[27] Report No. 502, 44 Cong., 2 Sess., p. 117.
[28] Douglas Report, pp. 16, 77, 106, 117–159, 558; Bruce Report, pp.
29, 196; Leipold's letter in *National Republican*, April 22, 1876.

Randall, of the House of Representatives, asking
for legislation which would permit the payment
of five per cent interest on bank funds deposited
in the United States Treasury. They also asked
that the bank building be purchased by the
United States government. The balances in the
Treasury for five years had been: December 31,
1874, $143,526.60; December 31, 1875, $156-
867.34; December 30, 1876, $253,479.08; Dec-
cember 31, 1877, $376,893.30; November 30,
1878, $230,826.36.[29]

It was a long time after the bank got into
difficulties before the depositors received any of
their money. There were numerous preferred
claims which had to be settled, and these payments took much of the ready money for the
first year. Then, as soon as there were enough
funds, a dividend was declared, and the money
distributed among the depositors. In this connection Purvis and Creswell performed most of
their work—at signing checks. A proposition to
have the government depositories distribute the
money was objected to by those members of Congress who believed that the government should
accept no responsibility whatever; so the checks
had to be written and sent to the depositors
through the mails. Under the administration of
the commissioners three dividends were declared:
20 per cent on November 1, 1875; 10 per cent
on March 20, 1878; 10 per cent on September 1,
1880. A 20 per cent dividend amounted to
$593,239.30.[30]

[29] Bruce Report, Appendix, pp. 7–9.
[30] *Sen. Ex. Doc.* No. 10, 45 Cong., 3 Sess.; *Bankers' Magazine*, July,
1881; Report of Commissioners, December 14, 1874. Among the preferred claims were those of depositors who had made deposits after
June 20, 1874.

When the commissioners were ready to pay a
dividend, the depositors were notified through
the press, especially through the Negro papers,
from the Negro pulpits, and, in the large cities,
by posters. Yet, although every means of finding
the depositors was taken, many of them could
never be located. When the average small depositor found that he could not draw out the
money as he wanted it, he decided that it was
forever lost, and numbers went away from their
old homes leaving no address and could not be
traced.

The reports published after several years
showed that as a rule only the principal depositors profited by the commissioners' distributions.
It was also explained that many who received
the first dividend were under the impression that
they had received all that had not been lost. In
1881, after three dividends had been declared,
it was found that of the 1875 dividend, $39,-
248.24 due to 31,967 depositors had not been
claimed, an average of $1.20 each; of the 1878
dividend, $30,927.26 due to 36,078 depositors
remained unclaimed, an average of 85 cents each;
of the 1880 dividend, $54,539.59 due to 40,000
depositors was not claimed. The average amount
now due from the three dividends to each of the
40,000 depositors was $3.40. In other words,
most of the small deposits were not claimed but
given up as lost, only the larger ones being called
for.[31] The payment of these small claims was
barred by an act of Congress in 1881, but later

[31] *Bankers' Magazine*, July, 1881; Bruce Report, p. 6; Reports of
the Commissioners, 1874–1880.

all claims were again admitted. The six years' work of the commissioners had resulted in the payment of 40 per cent in dividends, in reducing the accounts to fairly good order, and in the disposal of most of the property belonging to the bank.

Chapter VIII

THE AFFAIRS OF THE BANK UNDER THE COMPTROLLER OF THE CURRENCY

BOARD OF COMMISSIONERS ABOLISHED

THE necessity for changing the administration of the affairs of the bank had long been obvious and Congress was at last convinced. The administration of the three commissioners was too expensive—from 1874 to 1879 it had cost $355,994.77; they lacked full authority to dispose of the property of the bank, and their unedifying personal disputes brought discredit upon their work. So in 1881, partly as a result of the Bruce investigation, Congress abolished the board of commissioners and made the Comptroller of the Currency a commissioner to close out the business. He was allowed a salary of $1,000 to be taken from the funds of the bank; thus a saving of $8,000 a year in salaries alone was effected.[1]

DUTIES OF THE COMPTROLLER

By this act of Congress the funds collected by the Comptroller were to be placed in the United States Treasury and were to draw interest; when dividends were to be declared, he was to pay the

[1] Acts of February 21, 1881 and April 5, 1882.

depositors with government checks through United States depositories; he was given full authority to sell the remaining property and to wind up all business; and wherever it was possible he was to begin prosecution against former officials and trustees who were charged with violations of the laws safeguarding the bank.

The Comptroller disposed at once of all property that could be sold and paid a dividend of 15 per cent on June 1, 1882, and one of 7 per cent on May 12, 1883, making a total of 62 per cent returned to depositors. In 1882 he sold the bank building in Washington to the United States government for $250,000. To December 1, 1909, $1,731,854.01 had been repaid to depositors and $1,208,071.21 was still due. The government then had $7,991.58 belonging to the bank, but there was little likelihood that this balance would increase.[2] No prosecutions of former officials were undertaken.

THE DEMAND FOR RELIEF OF DEPOSITORS

As soon as it was seen that the bank had failed because of improper management a widespread demand arose that the government reimburse the depositors. From every southern state, from all the cities where branches were located, from Negro church congregations, from southern state legislatures, both Radical and Democratic, came memorials demanding that Congress make good the losses. The petitions asserted that the

[2] Hoffman, *Race Traits*, p. 290; Reports of the Commissioner, 1881-1909. Circular letters now (1927) sent out by the Comptroller's office state that there are no more funds. For table of dividends see Appendix pp. 141-143.

government was responsible because it had chartered the bank, had provided for Federal inspection, and had secured its funds by investment in United States bonds, and because its officials were usually government officials. All the advertising done by the bank had made it appear as an institution of the government, and the Negroes had generally understood that they were giving their money to the government for safe keeping.[3]

Men of note took the position that the United States should stand between the depositors and the loss of their savings. Frederick Douglass maintained that the government should make good the loss because it had allowed the bank to be considered a government institution and a part of the Freedmen's Bureau, and through neglect of supervision had allowed it to fail.[4] General Howard, trustee of the bank and formerly commissioner of the Freedmen's Bureau, who had permitted and encouraged the close connection between the bank and the Bureau, declared that the work of the former was done under the guarantee of the United States, and that therefore the government should hold itself responsible to the depositors.[5]

[3] *Ho. Misc. Doc.* No. 29, 43 Cong., 2 Sess.; *Ho. Report* No. 58, 43 Cong., 2 Sess.; *Cong. Globe*, 1874–1876. Shaler, *The Neighbor*, p. 170, makes a statement which shows that others than Negroes believed that the bank was connected with the government.

[4] Bruce Report, Appendix, p. 45.

[5] Bruce Report, p. 273. As indicating the close relation between the Freedmen's Bureau and the Freedmen's Savings Bank the following facts are significant: In 1872 the records of the Freedmen's Bureau were collected in Washington. Among these quantities of papers were found which belonged to the Freedmen's Savings Bank. These papers included certificates of soldiers, bounty registers, receipts for bounty, registers of

The several Comptrollers of the Currency who after 1881 had charge of the affairs of the defunct bank repeatedly recommended legislation in favor of the depositors. Comptroller John J. Knox declared in 1882 that the United States government had "assumed a quasi responsibility" by its negligence in incorporating and afterwards in failing to inspect the bank, as well as by permitting a close connection with the Freedmen's Bureau. He recommended that the losses to the depositors be paid out of the "overflowing Treasury" of the United States.[6] In 1885, H. W. Cannon, the next Comptroller, renewed his predecessor's recommendations and said, "It seems impossible for these people to realize that they are to be deprived of . . . a portion of their earnings, which years ago they labored so hard to acquire and save. Thousands of them to this day believe that the dividends paid to them by the commissioners are but the interest on their deposits, and that sooner or later their original deposits will be returned to them. No explanation seems to convince them to the contrary, and calls are made daily both orally and in writing for their money. Most of its branches were presided over by the commissioned and uniformed officers of the government."[7]

During Cleveland's first administration W. L. Trenholm, southern Democrat, then Comp-

claims, letter files, etc. They came from the branch banks at Wilmington, Charleston, Mobile, Savannah, Jacksonville, Tallahassee and Beaufort.— Report of Thomas M. Vincent, A. A. G. in *Ho. Ex. Doc.* No. 59, 43 Cong., 2 Sess.

[6] *Sen. Misc. Doc.* No. 10, 47 Cong., 2 Sess.; *Ho. Misc. Doc.* No. 10, 48 Cong., 1 Sess.

[7] *Ho. Misc. Doc.* No. 7, 48 Cong., 2 Sess., and No. 18, 49 Cong., 1 Sess.

troller, renewed the recommendation for the relief of the Negroes, and put their case more strongly than it had ever before been stated. As proving the moral responsibility of the government he again called attention to the identity of bank officials and Bureau officials, to the advertising literature which emphasized the semi-official status of the institution, to other facts which led the depositors to believe the bank under the care of the government, such as the absorption of the three army savings banks and the endorsement by Howard and Lincoln, and to the terms of the charter itself. And so it continued under Republican and Democrat until 1908.[8]

At various times the matter of compensating the depositors came before Congress. In 1875 a House committee reported that the government was in no way responsible for the debts of the Freedmen's Bank.[9] After the Bruce investigation in 1880 the question of assuming the losses of the depositors again came before Congress, and in 1883 John R. Lynch, a Negro congressman from Mississippi, reported from the Committee on Education and Labor a bill to appropriate $969,000 to compensate the depositors. The report stated that while the government was not legally bound to reimburse the depositors "the circumstances that were connected with the inauguration and management of the bank were of such a character as to make the government

[8] *Ho. Misc. Doc.* No. 34, 49 Cong., 2 Sess., and No. 33, 51 Cong., 1 Sess.; Annual Reports of the Comptroller as Commissioner, 1889, 1906, 1907 and 1908.

[9] *Ho. Report*, No. 58, 43 Cong., 2 Sess.

morally and equitably responsible to its creditors, and it should, therefore, reimburse them for any losses they have sustained in its failure." A minority report by Representative Money, of Mississippi, maintained that there was no warrant in law for paying such a claim, and that such a precedent would be extremely embarassing to the government.[10]

President Cleveland, in his message of 1886, reviewed the history of the bank and declared that to assume the losses was a "plain duty which the government owes to the depositors, and that the latter should be paid by the government upon principles of equity and fairness."[11] In pursuance of the President's suggestion a bill was introduced in 1888 appropriating money to pay the claims of the depositors. But after passing the Senate it failed in the House.[12]

In 1907 Senator Gallinger introduced a bill to reimburse the depositors. The bill again passed the Senate but failed in the House.[13] In 1910 the matter was again brought before Congress by Representative Austin of Tennessee but this effort excited very little interest.[14]

Since 1910 there has been no serious discussion of paying the depositors. Those who were in favor of paying the losses of the Negroes in 1875 no longer urged it for various reasons: The de-

[10] *Ho. Report*, No. 1901, 47 Cong., 2 Sess.

[11] *Messages and Papers of the Presidents*, VIII, 525.

[12] *Ho. Report*, No. 3199, 50 Cong., 1 Sess.

[13] Sen. Bill 48, 60 Cong., 1 Sess.

[14] See Banking and Currency Committee, Hearings in January, 1910, on House Bill 8776 to reimburse depositors of the Freedmen's Savings and Trust Company. Extracts from this document are given in the Appendix, p. 159.

positors were now dead, or scattered and difficult to find, especially those who had most needed aid; if appropriations should now be made, most of the claims would fall into the hands of speculators; and to the members of Congress it seemed a bad precedent to set, even if warrant in law could be found for it.

ESTIMATE OF THE BANK

The chain of savings banks for Negroes throughout the southern states gave promise of being a strong support, moral as well as financial, to those just emerging from slavery. Around each branch centered the forces which made for the economic and social elevation of the race. Thrift was inculcated and habits of saving were formed. Self-respect and pride in achievement were developed. Negro business men were being trained, and thousands of depositors were being taught to forego present pleasure for future good.

The following quotations from Negro writers will show the opinion of the leaders of the race in regard to the unfortunate effects of the failure. Brawley in his *Short History of the American Negro*[15] says: "This institution made a really remarkable start in the development of thrift among Negroes, and its failure, involving the loss of the first savings of hundreds of ex-slaves, was as disastrous in its moral as it was in its immediate financial consequences." Du Bois says:[16] "Not even ten additional years of slavery

[15] Pp. 126–127
[16] *Souls of Black Folk*, p. 36.

could have done so much to throttle the thrift
of the freedmen as the mismanagement and
bankruptcy of the series of savings banks chartered by the Nation for their special aid."
Booker T. Washington says of the results:
"When they found that they had lost or been
swindled out of their little savings they lost
faith in savings banks, and it was a long time
after this before it was possible to mention a
savings bank for Negroes without some reference
being made to the disaster of the Freedmen's
Bank."[17]

[17] *Story of the Negro*, II, 214.

APPENDIX

1. LAWS, 1865, 1870, 1874

ACT OF INCORPORATION, APPROVED MARCH 3, 1865

Be it enacted by the Senate and House of Representatives of the United States of America in Congress assembled, That Peter Cooper, William C. Bryant, A. A. Low, S. B. Chittenden, Charles H. Marshall, William A. Booth, Gerritt Smith, William A. Hall, William Allen, John Jay, Abraham Baldwin, A. S. Barnes, Hiram Barney, Seth B. Hunt, Samuel Holmes, Charles Collins, R. R. Graves, Walter S. Griffith, A. H. Wallis, D. S. Gregory, J. W. Alvord, George Whipple, A. S. Hatch, Walter T. Hatch, E. A. Lambert, W. G. Lambert, Roe Lockwood, R. H. Manning, R. W. Ropes, Albert Woodruff, and Thomas Denney, of New York; John M. Forbes, William Claflin, S. G. Howe, George L. Stearns, Edward Atkinson, A. A. Lawrence, and John M. S. Williams, of Massachusetts; Edward Harris and Thomas Davis, of Rhode Island; Stephen Calwell, J. Wheaton Smith, Francis E. Cope, Thomas Webster, B. S. Hunt, and Henry Samuel, of Pennsylvania; Edward Harwood, Adam Poe, Levi Coffin, J. M. Walden, of Ohio; and their successors, are constituted a body corporate in the city of Washington, in the District of Columbia, by the name of the Freedmen's Savings and Trust Company, and by that name may sue and be sued in any court of the United States.

Sec. 2 . . . the persons named in the first section of this act shall be the first trustees of the corporation, and all vacancies by death, resignation, or otherwise in the office of trustees shall be filled by the board, by ballot, without unnecessary delay, and at least ten votes shall be necessary for the election of any trustee. The trustees shall hold a regular meeting at least once in each month

131

to receive reports of their officers on the affairs of the
corporation, and to transact such business as may be
necessary; and any trustee omitting to attend the regular
meetings of the board for six months in succession may
thereupon be considered as having vacated his place, and
a successor may be elected to fill the same.

Sec. 3 . . . the business of the corporation shall be
managed and directed by the board of trustees, who shall
elect from their number a president and two vice-presidents, and may appoint such other officers as they may
see fit; nine of the trustees, of whom the president or one
of the vice-presidents shall be one, shall form a quorum
for the transaction of business at any regular or adjourned
meeting of the board of trustees; and the affirmative vote
of at least seven members of the board shall be requisite in
making any order for, or authorizing the investment of
any moneys, or the sale or transfer of any stock or securities belonging to the corporation, or the appointment
of any officer receiving any salary therefrom.

Sec. 4 . . . the board of trustees of the corporation
shall have power, from time to time, to make and establish
such by-laws and regulations as they shall judge proper
with regard to the elections of officers and their respective
functions, and generally for the management of the affairs
of the corporation, provided such by-laws and regulations
are not repugnant to this act, or to the Constitution or
laws of the United States.

Sec. 5 . . . the general business and object of the corporation hereby created shall be to receive on deposit
such sums of money, as may from time to time be offered
therefor, by or on behalf of persons heretofore held in
slavery in the United States, or their descendants, and
investing the same in stocks, bonds, Treasury notes, or
other securities of the United States.

Sec. 6 . . . it shall be the duty of the trustees of the
corporation to invest, as soon as practicable, in the securities named in the next preceding section, all sums
received by them beyond an available fund not exceeding
one third of the total amount of deposits with the corporation, at the discretion of the trustees, which available

funds may be kept by the trustees to meet current payments of the corporation, and may, by them, be left on deposit, at interest or otherwise, or in such available form as the trustees may direct.

Sec. 7 . . . the corporation may, under such regulations as the board of trustees shall, from time to time, prescribe, receive any deposit hereby authorized to be received upon such trusts and for such purposes, not contrary to the laws of the United States, as may be indicated in writing by the depositor, such writing to be subscribed by the depositor and acknowledged or proved before any officer in the civil or military service of the United States, the certificate of which acknowledgment or proof shall be indorsed on the writing; and the writing, so acknowledged or proved, shall accompany such deposit and be filed among the papers of the corporation, and be carefully preserved therein, and may be read in evidence in any court or before any judicial officer of the United States, without further proof; and the certificate of acknowledgment or proof shall be *prima facie* evidence only of the due execution of such writing.

Sec. 8 . . . all sums received on deposit shall be repaid to such depositor when required, at such time, with such interest, not exceeding seven per centum per annum, and under such regulations as the board of trustees shall, from time to time, prescribe, which regulations shall be posted up in some conspicuous place in the place where the business of the corporation shall be transacted, but shall not be altered so as to affect any deposit previously made.

Sec. 9 . . . all trusts upon which, and all purposes for which, any deposit shall be made, and which shall be indicated in the writing to accompany such deposit, shall be faithfully performed by the corporation, unless the performing of the same is rendered impossible.

Sec. 10 . . . when any depositor shall die, the funds remaining on deposit with the corporation to his credit and all accumulations thereof, shall belong and be paid to the personal representatives of such depositor, in case he shall have left a last will and testament, and in default of a last will and testament, or of any person qualifying under a last will and testament, competent to act as executor, the corporation shall be entitled, in respect to the funds so remaining on deposit to the credit of any such depositor, to administration thereon in preference to all other persons, and letters of administration shall be granted to the corporation accordingly in the manner prescribed by law in respect to granting of letters of administration, with the will annexed, and in cases of intestacy.

Sec. 11 . . . in the case of the death of any depositor, whose deposit shall not be held upon any trust created pursuant to the provisions herein before contained, or where it may prove impossible to execute such trust, it shall be the duty of the corporation to make diligent efforts to ascertain and discover whether such deceased depositor has left a husband, wife, or children surviving, and the corporation shall keep a record of the efforts so made, and of the results thereof; and in case no person lawfully entitled thereto shall be discovered, or shall appear, or claim the funds remaining to the credit of such depositor before the expiration of two years from the death of such depositor, it shall be lawful for the corporation to hold and invest such funds as a separate trust fund, to be applied, with the accumulations thereof, to the education and improvement of persons heretofore held in slavery, or their descendants, being inhabitants of the United States, in such manner and through such agencies as the board of trustees shall deem best calculated to effect that object; *Provided*, That if any depositor be not heard from within five years from the date of his last deposit, the trustees shall advertise the same in some paper of general circulation in the State where the principal office of the company is established, and also in the State where the depositor was last heard from; and if, within two years thereafter, such depositor shall not appear, nor a husband, wife, or child of such depositor, to claim his deposits, they shall be used by the board of trustees as hereinbefore provided for in this section.

Sec. 12 . . . no president, vice-president, trustee, officer, or servant of the corporation shall, directly or indirectly, borrow the funds of the corporation or its deposits, or in any manner use the same, or any part thereof, except to pay necessary expenses, under the direction of the board of trustees. All certificates or other evidences of deposit made by the proper officers shall be as binding on the corporation as if they were made under their common seal. It shall be the duty of the trustees to regulate the rate of interest allowed to the depositors so that they shall receive, as nearly as may be, a ratable proportion of all the profits of the corporation after deducting all necessary expenses: *Provided, however,* That the trustees may allow to depositors, to the amount of five hundred dollars or upwards, one per centum less than the amount allowed others: *And provided, also,* Whenever it shall appear that, after the payment of the usual interest to depositors, there is in the possession of the corporation an excess of profits over the liabilities amounting to ten per centum upon the deposits, such excess shall be invested for the security of the depositors in the corporation; and thereafter, at each annual examination of the affairs of the corporation, any surplus over and above such ten per centum shall, in addition to the usual interest, be divided ratably among the depositors in such manner as the board of trustees shall direct.

Sec. 13 . . . whenever any deposits shall be made by any minor, the trustees of the corporation may, at their discretion, pay to such depositor such sum as may be due to him, although no guardian shall have been appointed for such minor, or the guardian of such minor shall not have authorized the drawing of the same; and the check, receipt, or acquittance of such minor shall be as valid as if the same were executed by a guardian of such minor. And whenever any deposits shall have been made by married women, the trustees may repay the same of their own receipts.

Sec. 14 . . . the trustees shall not directly or indirectly receive any payment or emolument for their services as such, except the president and vice-president.

Sec. 15 . . . the president, vice-president, and subordinate officers and agents of the corporation shall respectively give such security for their fidelity and good conduct as the board of trustees may from time to time require, and the board shall fix the salaries of such officers and agents.

Sec. 16 . . . the books of the corporation shall, at all times during the hours of business, be open for inspection and examination to such persons as Congress shall designate or appoint.

THE AMENDMENT OF 1870

Be it enacted . . . That the fifth section of the act entitled "An act to incorporate the Freedmen's Savings and Trust Company," approved March third, eighteen hundred and sixty-five, be, and the same is hereby, amended by adding thereto, at the end thereof, the words following: "and to the extent of one half in bonds or notes, secured by mortgage on real estate in double the value of the loan; and the corporation is also authorized hereby to hold and improve the real estate now owned by it in the city of Washington, to wit, the west half of lot number three; all of lots four, five, six, seven, and the south half of lot number eight, in square number two hundred and twenty-one, as laid out and recorded in the original plats or plan of said city; *Provided*, That said corporation shall not use the principal of any deposits made with it for the purpose of such improvement."

Sec. 2 . . . Congress shall have the right to alter or repeal this amendment at any time.

ACT OF JUNE 20, 1874

Be it enacted . . . That the act of Congress approved March third, eighteen hundred and sixty-five, entitled "An act to incorporate the Freedmen's Savings and Trust Company," be, and the same is hereby, so amended that hereafter it shall be the duty of the trustees and officers of said company to make loans, to the extent of one half the deposits by them received, upon bonds or notes secured by first mortgages or deeds of trust upon unencumbered real estate, situate in the vicinity of the agency or branch of said company from which such deposits are

received, worth, upon cash appraisement, at least double
the amount of money loaned thereon. And the borrower
shall at his own expense, or the bank shall at the expense
of the borrower, keep the buildings upon said property
insured in some good and solvent company, to the amount
of one half of their cash value, for the benefit of the
Freedmen's Savings and Trust Company. The other half
they shall invest in United States bonds, or keep on deposit
in some national bank such sums as may be necessary to
meet current payments.

Sec. 2 . . . it shall be the duty of said trustees and
officers of said company to collect, as speedily as may be
done without prejudice to the interest of the depositors,
all sums of money by them loaned upon real estate outside
of the States from which received; and when collected,
and as the same may be collected, they shall loan such
funds as directed in the first section of this act.

Sec. 3 . . . when it shall appear that the interests of
the depositors may require it, it shall be lawful for the
trustees of the corporation, by and with the advice and
consent of the Secretary of the Treasury, at any time to
close any of the agencies or branches of the corporation
paying to the depositors of such agencies or branches a
pro rata amount of the principal and interest which may
be due them and also a ratable proportion of any surplus
which may have accumulated under the provisions of section eight of this act. And whenever it may be deemed
advisable, or when so ordered by Congress, the general
business and affairs of the corporation shall, in like manner, be closed up by the trustees of the corporation, as
provided for in section seven herein.

Sec. 4 . . . said trustees and officers of said company
shall not loan to any person or company at any time more
than ten thousand dollars of the funds of said trust
company.

Sec. 5 . . . every officer, clerk, or agent of the company
who shall embezzle, abstract, or wilfully misapply any of
the money, funds, or credits of the company, issue or put
forth any pass-book, certificate of deposit, or other evidence of indebtedness, draw any order, bill of exchange,

mortgage, or confess any judgment or decree whereby said
company may be charged with any liability, or be deprived of any of its assets, or shall make any false entry
in any book, report, or statement of the company, or
wilfully deceive any officer of the company, or any agent
appointed to examine the affairs or condition of the company, shall be deemed guilty of misdemeanor, and upon
conviction thereof, shall be punished by imprisonment for
a period not exceeding five years.

Sec. 6 . . . hereafter the officers or agents of said trust
company shall not pay interest on the deposits exceeding
five per centum.

Sec. 7 . . . whenever it shall be deemed advisable by
the trustees of said corporation to close up its entire business, then they shall select three competent men, not connected with the previous management of the institution
and approved by the Secretary of the Treasury, to be
known and styled commissioners, whose duty it shall be
to take charge of all the property and effects of said
Freedmen's Savings and Trust Company, close up the
principal and subordinate branches, collect from the
branches all the deposits they have on hand, and proceed
to collect all sums due said company, and dispose of all
the property owned by said company, as speedily as the
interests of the corporation require, and to distribute the
proceeds among the creditors pro rata, according to
their respective amounts; they shall make a pro rata
dividend whenever they have funds enough to pay twenty
per centum of the claims of the depositors. Said commissioners, before they proceed to act, shall execute a joint
bond to the United States, with good sureties, in the penal
sum of one hundred thousand dollars, conditioned for the
faithful discharge of their duties as commissioners aforesaid, and shall take an oath to faithfully and honestly
perform their duties as such, which bonds shall be executed
in presence of the Secretary of the Treasury, be approved
by him, and by him safely kept; and whenever said trustees shall file with the Secretary of the Treasury a certified
copy of the order appointing said commissioners, and they
shall have executed the bonds and taken the oath aforesaid, then said commissioners shall be invested with the

legal title to all of said property of said company, for the purpose of this act, and shall have full power and authority to sell the same, and make deeds of conveyance to any and all of the real estate sold by them to the purchasers. Said commissioners may employ such agents as are necessary to assist them in closing up said company, and pay them a reasonable compensation for their services out of the funds of said company; and said commissioners shall retain out of said funds a reasonable compensation for their trouble, to be fixed by the Secretary of the Treasury and the Comptroller of the Currency and not exceeding three thousand dollars each per annum. Said commissioners shall deposit all sums collected by them in the Treasury of the United States until they make a pro rata distribution of the same.

Sec. 8 . . . from and after the passage of this act and until the first day of July, eighteen hundred and seventy-five, all the deposits made in said Trust Company shall be held by the trustees of said company as special deposits, and any investments made of said deposits shall be made and held for the use and benefit of said depositors only; and it shall be the duty of said trustees on or before the first day of July, eighteen hundred and seventy-five, to make a full and complete statement of all the assets and liabilities of said company and lay the same before the Secretary of the Treasury, and if said Secretary and the trustees shall at that time after investigating the condition of said company believe the same to be solvent then the trustees and said Secretary shall issue an order declaring that thereafter all deposits shall be general; but said order shall in nowise affect the special deposits, unless said depositors shall in writing consent that said special deposits shall become general deposits. But if the Secretary and trustees of said company shall on the first day of July, eighteen hundred and seventy-five, after the examination aforesaid doubt the propriety of making the deposits thereafter general then the deposits made shall still be special until the first day of July, eighteen hundred and seventy-six, or until the said Secretary and trustees deem it prudent to make said deposits general.

2. STATEMENTS OF DIVIDENDS AND PAYMENTS

1. STATEMENT OF DIVIDENDS PAID TO 1900

BASED UPON REPORTS OF THE COMPTROLLER OF THE CURRENCY

At the time of the failure of the company in 1874 there were
61,131 depositors, to whom there was due............$2,939,925.22

Five dividends were declared, as follows:
- (1) 20 per cent, November 1, 1875................... $587,985.04
- (2) 10 per cent, March 20, 1878.................... 293,992.52
- (3) 10 per cent, September 1, 1880................... 293,992.52
- (4) 15 per cent, June 1, 1882....................... 440,988.78
- (5) 7 per cent, May 12, 1883....................... 205,794.76

Aggregating 62 per cent, and amounting to............$1,822,753.62

Of this amount there was called for, and
paid...............................$1,638,259.49

Less unclaimed checks returned and cancelled...........................   735.57   1,637,523.92

Leaving unpaid and barred by act of February 17, 1881.. $185,229.70

Of this amount there was revived by the act of February
17, 1883...................................... $17,481.10

Of which amount there has been paid.....$ 10,773.37

Less unclaimed checks returned and cancelled...........................   55.29   10,718.08

Leaving uncalled for, but which will be paid if presented,
under act of March 3, 1899........................ $ 6,763.02

Total payments on all accounts to date have been as follows:
- On account of dividends declared...................$1,637,523.92
- Under act of February 17, 1883...................... 10,718.08
- Under act of March 3, 1899.......................... 7,214.21
- Special deposits and preferred claims................. 73,565.03

Total (to 1900)................................$1,729,021.24

Total (to 1909)................................ 1,731,854.01

2. TABLE SHOWING TOTAL PAYMENTS TO THE CREDITORS OF THE FREEDMEN'S SAVINGS AND TRUST COMPANY TO 1900

Branches	First dividend		Second dividend		Third dividend		Fourth dividend		Final dividend		Total payments at each branch	Less unclaimed checks returned and destroyed	Total amount of claims paid
	No. of claimants	Nov. 1, 1875, 20 per cent	No. of claimants	Mar. 20, 1878, 10 per cent	No. of claimants	Sept. 1, 1880, 10 per cent	No. of claimants	June 1, 1882, 15 per cent	No. of claimants	May 12, 1883, 7 per cent			
Alexandria, Va.	226	$2,694.65	207	$1,338.38	197	$1,318.07	173	$1,974.00	136	$870.88	$8,195.98	$11.05	$8,184.93
Atlanta, Ga.	554	5,093.89	424	2,238.82	362	2,219.36	318	3,163.20	246	1,362.94	14,078.21	3.34	14,074.87
Augusta, Ga.	1,505	17,012.84	1,300	8,255.63	1,212	8,161.09	1,134	12,183.16	1,057	5,626.94	51,239.66		51,239.66
Baltimore, Md.	2,411	54,788.02	2,193	26,930.55	2,036	26,177.06	1,890	38,794.54	1,671	17,445.78	164,135.95	30.52	164,105.43
Beaufort, S. C.	516	4,930.78	439	2,330.62	395	2,233.38	337	3,276.75	287	1,377.28	14,148.81		14,148.81
Charleston, S. C.	3,024	46,649.32	2,823	22,430.33	2,541	22,016.86	2,352	33,156.65	2,104	15,077.83	139,330.99		139,330.99
Columbus, Miss.	124	943.09	91	417.19	57	363.59	49	519.62	43	236.40	2,479.89		2,479.89
Columbia, Tenn.	338	3,365.85	311	1,648.66	282	1,605.06	269	2,412.60	180	970.63	10,002.80		10,002.80
Huntsville, Ala.	328	6,468.84	300	3,175.52	280	3,134.41	280	4,706.04	263	2,172.70	19,657.51		19,657.51
Jacksonville, Fla.	576	6,721.67	487	3,249.66	400	2,927.59	350	4,260.55	306	1,911.14	19,070.61	9.73	19,060.88
Lexington, Ky.	347	6,115.44	287	2,686.30	254	2,679.44	226	3,750.52	207	1,631.41	16,863.11	2.92	16,860.19
Little Rock, Ark.	115	2,504.12	95	1,187.83	90	1,171.43	93	1,748.80	86	772.35	7,384.53		7,384.53
Louisville, Ky.	1,376	24,529.46	1,216	11,911.56	1,089	11,570.48	918	16,870.01	792	7,620.77	72,502.28	38.09	72,464.19
Lynchburg, Va.	299	2,880.61	256	1,380.89	220	1,335.98	197	1,957.75	155	789.68	8,344.91	12.53	8,332.38
Macon, Ga.	716	9,549.62	560	4,635.52	479	4,476.04	429	6,532.09	365	2,963.05	28,161.32	3.52	28,157.80
Memphis, Tenn.	756	16,697.02	687	8,141.44	564	7,559.55	512	11,198.00	422	4,889.29	48,485.30	8.90	48,476.40
Mobile, Ala.	939	15,417.26	814	7,515.41	763	7,322.29	686	10,713.27	584	4,853.97	45,822.20	25.25	45,796.95
Natchez, Miss.	106	3,735.95	96	1,843.19	83	1,742.06	84	2,713.50	73	1,197.92	11,232.62		11,232.62
Nashville, Tenn.	804	13,823.03	644	6,644.78	564	6,395.82	514	9,320.90	450	4,231.57	40,416.10		40,416.10
New Bern, N. C.	576	6,218.01	468	2,922.94	427	2,920.66	396	4,381.96	349	2,030.10	18,473.67	5.59	18,468.08
New Orleans, La.	1,314	43,631.56	1,062	20,944.91	962	20,337.62	890	29,725.92	767	12,973.58	127,613.59	24.51	127,589.08
New York, N. Y.	1,529	62,026.87	1,318	29,996.19	1,174	28,577.67	1,151	42,614.06	1,021	19,125.13	182,339.92	1.51	182,338.41
Norfolk, Va.	1,296	20,346.23	1,136	9,665.12	984	9,208.05	935	13,678.41	837	6,131.54	59,029.35	521.99	58,507.36
Philadelphia, Pa.	719	13,685.82	632	6,720.74	568	6,585.68	523	9,607.97	471	4,377.69	40,977.90		40,977.90
Raleigh, N. C.	579	5,739.51	455	2,716.76	390	2,595.93	324	3,725.69	276	1,645.47	16,423.36	8.32	16,415.04
Richmond, Va.	2,000	27,406.81	1,732	13,280.23	1,527	12,765.84	1,475	19,222.49	1,296	8,797.43	81,472.80	2.17	81,470.63
Savannah, Ga.	1,706	25,493.03	1,468	12,256.85	1,383	12,092.32	1,314	17,993.59	1,130	7,984.93	75,820.72	.25	75,820.47

Shreveport, La........	346	5,680.59	300	2,703.65	240	2,591.62	196	3,517.87	149	1,450.82	15,944.55	6.46	15,938.09
St. Louis, Mo........	421	9,989.68	347	4,624.41	304	4,396.13	280	6,482.52	258	2,863.14	28,355.88	6.06	28,349.82
Tallahassee, Fla......	339	4,840.47	283	2,329.38	224	2,240.23	205	3,321.53	181	1,486.85	14,218.46	2.87	14,214.59
Vicksburg, Miss......	633	14,311.51	535	6,477.22	412	5,888.29	393	8,981.33	312	3,892.41	39,550.76	....	39,550.76
Wilmington, N. C....	780	7 653.04	641	3,599.45	516	3,468.01	488	5,119.42	411	2,309.35	22,149.27	3.89	22,140.88
Washington, D. C....	2,676	63,381.08	2,444	31,191.04	2,292	30,886.70	2,136	45,979.80	1,879	20,785.18	192,203.80	1.60	192,202.20
Miscellaneous........	22	1,004.41	14	292.17	9	260.87	10	392.20	10	183.03	2,132.68	....	2,132.68
Total dividends paid	29,996	555,360.08	26,065	267,683.34	23,280	259,123.18	21,527	383,996.71	18,774	172,096.18	1,638,259.49	735.57	1,637,523.92
Barred claims, section 1, act February 17, 1883..........	....	....	....	....	....	....	....	....	....	....	5,215.45	36.77	5,178.68
Barred claims, section 2, act February 17, 1883..........	....	....	....	....	....	....	....	....	....	....	5,557.92	18.52	5,539.40
Barred claims under act March 3, 1899..	....	....	....	....	....	....	....	....	....	....	7,214.21	....	7,214.21
Special deposits and preferred claims....	....	....	....	....	....	....	....	....	....	....	73,565.03	....	73,565.03
Total.............	....	....	....	....	....	....	....	....	....	....	1,729,812.10	790.86	1,729,021.24

3. SPECIMENS OF THE ADVERTISING LITERATURE

1. (BANK BOOK, OUTSIDE COVER, EDITION OF 1867)

NATIONAL SAVINGS BANK

FREEDMEN'S
SAVINGS AND TRUST COMPANY,
Chartered by Congress

PRINCIPAL OFFICE,
CORNER 19th STREET AND PENNSYLVANIA
AVENUE, WASHINGTON, D. C.
WASHINGTON BRANCH OFFICE,
AT THE SAME PLACE,

Where deposits will be received every business day from
9 A.M. to 3 P.M.

Branches also in New York, Baltimore, and all the
Principal Cities of the South and Southwest

"Tall oaks from little acorns grow."

"DESPISE NOT THE DAY OF SMALL THINGS."

2. (BOOKLET, 1869, p. 12)

Temperance Man.—A printer once determined that every time his fellow-workmen went out to drink beer during the working hours he would put in the bank the exact amount which he would have spent if he had gone out to drink. He kept to this resolution for five years. He then examined his bank account, and found that he had on deposit $521.86. In the five years he had not lost a day from ill health. Three out of five of his fellow-workmen had in the meantime become drunkards, were worthless as workmen, and were discharged. The water drinker then bought out the printing office, went on enlarging his business, and in twenty years from the time he began to put by his money, was worth $100,000.

3. (BOOKLET, 1867)

REASONS WHY YOU SHOULD ALL PUT MONEY IN THE SAVINGS BANK

1. *Because it is your surest way to get a start in life.* Thousands of rich men would have been poor all their lifetime had they not used the Savings Bank.

2. *Because, being your own masters, it is your duty to provide for your settlement in life, for your families, for sickness, and for old age.* You can in no way do this so well as by a monthly deposit in a good Savings Bank.

3. *It teaches you the value of money,* and prevents you from spending it foolishly.

4. *You should use this Bank* because it is conducted entirely by your best friends, and it is hoped you will, ere long, help to conduct it yourselves; and being authorized by Congress, and approved by the President of the United States, it is the safest place you can find for your money.

5. *It gives you character.* As soon as you become worth a little money or property, every one begins to respect you and ask your advice.

6. *It is a good example of thrift to your children,* whom you desire to see respected and prosperous citizens. They will be sure to imitate your example.

4. (PASS BOOK, 1867, THIRD PAGE OF COVER)

COLORED CITIZEN'S SAVINGS BANK
Chartered by Congress, March 3, 1865

ABRAHAM LINCOLN'S GIFT
to the
COLORED PEOPLE
His signature to the Bill one of the last acts of his life.

He gave EMANCIPATION, and then this
SAVINGS BANK
Your *freedom* and *prosperity* were in his heart united.

ECONOMY THE ROAD TO WEALTH.
SAVE YOUR MONEY!
Save the pennies, and the dollars will take
care of themselves

"I consider the Freedmen's Savings and Trust Company to be greatly needed by the Colored People, and have welcomed it as an auxiliary to the Freedmen's Bureau."

Maj. Gen'l. O. O. Howard.

5. (BOOKLET, 1867, p. 11)

CHILDREN IN THE SCHOOLS

There is a way for little children in the schools to have a part in the Bank.

Let teachers take some pretty envelopes from us, on which is printed "Savings Bank," and have one for each scholar; then let all the spare pennies, five cent and ten cent bills which the children can earn, be put in the envelope until they amount to one dollar.

This dollar will then be brought, by the teacher, to the cashier of the bank. The cashier will take the children's dollar and give them a *bank book* for it, and when they get another dollar in the same way to put in, it will be two *dollars*, and so on.

All the children of the colored people will, in this way, learn to save, and not to waste what they get, and will have money, when they want it, in the "Savings Bank." Some, who are very saving, will finally have a large sum to do good with, and for their mothers when they are sick; or to help buy a house and garden, where they and their parents can live very happily.

I know of two little boys who have ten dollars apiece in the Freedmen's Savings Bank, and they mean to have more than that.

6. (BOOKLET, 1867, pp. 7–10)

A FEW WORDS, COLORED PEOPLE

You have here presented to you the names of some of the best men in your country, who have gratuitously assumed the care and responsibility of a company for the safe-keeping and investment of your spare earnings.

You are now on the same footing, as to your legal rights, with all other people of this country. You get your wages for your labor, and no one can prevent you.

If you work hard you will earn money the same as other folks. Not one of you need remain poor if you are careful and do not spend money for candy, or whiskey, or costly clothes. As for food, cheap, hearty victuals—beef, fish, bread, coffee—will do for men and women better than pies, cakes, and such things which cost more money and give you less strength.

Tobacco and *Whiskey* are the two things which all men who are going to save money must neither touch nor taste.

Let us count the cost of a cigar and a glass of whiskey every working day. A mean cigar costs five cents, and the poorest glass of whiskey five cents, which makes ten cents.

Now, if instead of worse than wasting this, you would save it every day—*one Dime* per day—at the end of one year, of three hundred and twelve working days, amounts to thirty-one dollars and twenty cents. ($31.20)

How nice to have that much cash to put by at Christmas!

Now, what will you do with it? Will you put it away in an old stocking, or hide it in a crack in the floor, where bad folks may steal it, or the mice eat it up? Or, suppose it isn't stolen or eaten up by mice; if safe hid away it would be making nothing for you. It would be like the unfaithful steward's talent, which the Bible tells of! You know his Lord, when he came, condemned him for having hidden his talent in a napkin. He called him "a wicked and slothful servant."

Instead, then, of hiding your savings in a napkin, put it in the bank, where it will be making money for you. You will get, we will say, six per cent interest for it.

Now let us see how much a man, who saves ten cents every working day for ten years, will have if he puts it at interest:

The first year he will have..............$ 31.20

The second year he will have.......... 33.07

The third year he will have............ 35.05

The fourth year he will have........... 37.15

The fifth year he will have............. 39.38

The sixth year he will have............ 41.74

The seventh year he will have......... 44.24

The eighth year he will have........... 46.90

The ninth year he will have........... 49.71

The tenth year he will have........... 52.69

And at the end of ten years he will be worth in cash......................$411.13

And all this from saving the price of a mean cigar and a vile glass of liquor every day! There is no excuse for any healthy man being poor in this country. The richest men in it began by small savings. The merchant, Billy Gray, of Boston, saved his first dollar by carrying bricks. Then he added another and another to that, and saved the interest, and put that on interest, and at last had many millions of dollars.

But the worst of it is yet to tell: if you had spent the ten cents a day in tobacco and whiskey, you would not only not have had the $411.13 at the ten years' end, but also had bad habits. Very likely you would have become a drunkard, and spent not five but fifty cents a day, if you could get them, for the drunkard's cup. Your family would be ragged; your wife miserable, and perhaps heart-broken; your children growing up in vices, with no chance to learn to read or write.

But, on the other hand, the very fact of saving the money will bring with it the pleasure, pride in yourself, good habits, good health, a good name, steady employment. All people will trust you. Men will point you out and say—"There's a sober, hard-working, honest man, with money ahead; you can trust him." So, too, will your wife be proud of you, and your children will respect you and grow up willing and obedient. They will all join to aid you in saving. A pleasant strife will appear in your household to see who can do most toward adding to the father's savings, and by the time he had saved the sum I have mentioned, very likely they have all added $200 more.

But I have said nothing about the many chances which a man who has $500 ready cash in bank has to make it increase. I have just supposed a case of saving ten cents a day for ten years. Do you think any man would stop at that sum after trying it a short time? No; he would see chances to put his savings into some business of his own, and go on to buy and sell and get gain. He would not be content to work for hire all his life. He could buy his piece of land and become a thriving farmer! The earth would be working for him day and night. He would see flocks and herds grazing on his own pastures. He would drive his own horse and wagon to market. He would enlarge his fields by his gains. He would become a good citizen, giving freely to the school and church, and all things that make for peace and freedom and justice.

Thus good people live. Thus whole nations grow great. Thus, in smaller cities than this, men of toil have their five hundred thousand dollars, all having commenced by putting small sums in the savings bank. Take this good word then: Avoid bad habits, and put your savings in the bank.

7. (BOOKLET, 1869, p. 13)

How a Man Saves Money by Leaving Off Tobacco.—A man once found, on examining his expenses at the end of the year, that he had spent in the year—

For tobacco.............................$52
And for his family's bread................ 42

He said to himself, "I have wronged my family out of this $52. I will never touch the weed again." Up to this day he has not touched it. That was ten years ago. Now how much has this man saved?

In one year.............................$52
In ten years............................520

which with interest at the rate paid by the National Savings Bank, makes $678.09.

How to Get Rich.—If a boy at 15 years of age lays by ten cents a day in our Bank, when he is 21 years old he will be worth $257.01.

If a young girl should save one dollar a week, and put it in our Bank and keep on doing it for a year, she would have $53.70. In five years she would be worth, in cash, $297.20.

If a laboring man should put in the bank $10 a month,
In one year he would have..........$ 124.00
In five years....................... 686.40
In ten years........................ 1,565.93

A young man at the age of 17 determined to lay by and put in the National Savings Bank at interest One Dollar every week till he should reach the age of 27. At the age of 27 he married a wife and set up housekeeping. He had in clear cash $678.09. His wife then commenced to aid him. They determined to save one dollar a week. They did this for three years, when they were worth in cash, $1,123.74.

4. CIRCULARS ISSUED BY FREDERICK DOUGLASS

WHEN PRESIDENT OF THE FREEDMEN'S SAVINGS
AND TRUST COMPANY

(CIRCULAR NO. 1)

*To the Depositors of the Freedmen's Savings and Trust
Company:*

The recent legislation of Congress, so amending the charter of the Freedmen's Savings and Trust Company as to place the institution upon a broader and firmer basis and give to its trustees a larger measure of discretion and control of its management, may be well enough made the occasion for a brief statement of facts and circumstances which have a bearing upon the legislation in question and upon the future existence and success of the Freedmen's Bank.

It is very evident that Congress was animated in its legislation by a generous desire to conserve and strengthen an institution of known usefulness to the people in whose interest it was created.

In regard to the condition of this corporation, certain facts have already come to public knowledge through the publication of the report of Mr. Meigs, the bank examiner.

It is not necessary to disguise or explain away by false processes the facts therein stated. It is known that on the 1st of January, 1874, our liabilities exceeded our assets to the extent of $217,000, and it is also known that nothing has occurred since that time to materially diminish the space between assets and liabilities, though it is due to state that several considerable loans which were supposed at the time the report was made to be bad, have turned out to be good loans.

This deficit now admitted and never denied by the undersigned is very easily accounted for, and it may serve a good purpose to state the cause of its existence.

First. The managers of the "Freedmen's Savings and Trust Company" have unfortunately endeavored to make

the Freedmen's Bank compete with older and better established institutions of the kind in attracting and securing
a large amount of deposits, by holding out the inducement
of a larger percentage of interest than was warranted by
the earnings of the bank.

Of course any corporation, nation, or family which
spends more than it earns will in due time find its coffers
exhausted.

Second. Another cause of this deficit of $200,000 is found
in the fact that the former managers of the Freedmen's
Savings and Trust Company undertook to do too much
work in another direction; impressed as they were with
the sense of the many benefits of savings institutions
among the freedmen of the South, they were tempted into
a sort of banking missionary movement.

Third. It cannot be doubted that a third cause has in a
large measure operated against the success of the Freedmen's Bank, and this cause happens to be one which it is
most difficult to deal with,—because it is inherent in the
enterprise itself,—and one which no wisdom that the
managers of the bank can exercise can counteract or
remove.

This institution conspicuously and pre-eminently repre-
sents the idea of progress and elevation of a people who
are just now emerging from the ignorance, degradation,
and destitution entailed upon them by more than two
centuries of slavery. A people who are hated not because
they have injured others but because others have injured
them. This feeling of caste, this race malignity, has naturally enough taken about the same offense at the Freedmen's Bank as it did at the existence of the Freedmen's
Bureau. It is as desirous to destroy the former as it was
to destroy the latter.

Fourth. Still another and greater source of evil has been
the senseless runs made from time to time upon the bank.
These have compelled the withdrawal of large sums of
money from very safe and profitable investments, and
diverted the regular business of the bank from making
money for its depositors to the work of obtaining the
means of meeting the demands of these disastrous panics.

The Freedmen's Bank has been subjected to no less than three of these raids during the last eighteen months. The run made upon the bank by the failure of Jay Cooke & Co. cost us no less than $500,000, and required the withdrawal of a half million dollars from safe and profitable investments. Add to these causes the general prostration of business, the great loss of confidence to all moneyed institutions, the disturbed condition of affairs, especially in the District of Columbia, where most of our loans have been made, and you will easily understand why the Freedmen's Bank is now under a heavy strain, and found it necessary to seek protection in the recent amendments to its charter.

In respect to the future of the bank some of the main sources of danger and ruin have been entirely removed. The trustees, governed by an increasing concern for the safety of their depositors rather than for large profits in the way of interest, have abandoned their unwise competition with others in the offer of a high percentage of interest, and have now resolved to pay only such a rate as the net earnings of the bank will warrant them in paying. They have also given up their wild and visionary schemes of banking, and have abandoned the policy of establishing branches in remote corners of the country. They will now establish none where there is not a very strong likelihood of their becoming self-sustaining. Not only have they discarded the policy of extension, they have adopted the policy of closing up as speedily as is convenient and practicable the non-paying branches now in operation. They are not only for decreasing the number of branches but also the number of employees, and for reducing the salaries of their agents to the lowest point consistent with securing the services of good men. With this retrenchment of expenses, with wise and vigorous management, and with the returning confidence of our people, it is believed that the Freedmen's Savings and Trust Company, which has already been a powerful instrument in promoting the moral, social, and intellectual welfare of our people, will survive and flourish despite the machinations of its enemies.

The effect of the legislation recently enacted upon the bank will naturally inspire confidence. It is indirectly a strong indorsement of the honesty and ability of the trustees of the institution. It puts the destiny of the Freedmen's Savings and Trust Company more completely than heretofore within their power and discretion. It devises an honest method of keeping the institution in continued and successful operation, while it at the same time enables it to accomplish all the objects usually sought in suspension. It completely divorces the past from the present and future; it separates the old from the new, and allows the dead past to bury its dead; it aims to protect the new depositor from all the mistakes and misfortunes connected with the management and past condition of the bank. For the interests of the old depositors, it enables the trustees to hold their securities as long as may be necessary to reap the full amount of interest they are capable of drawing, and then allows the trustees to fill up the chasm which may exist between assets and liabilities. It puts it in the power of the officers and agents of the Freedmen's Savings and Trust Company to say with confidence and truth to all our old depositors, give us time and we will pay you every dollar due you from the company. To the new depositors it enables us to say with even more confidence, you may deposit with safety and profit. You are neither affected by past losses nor past mismanagement. Your money shall not be in any way mixed up with the old nor taken to pay old debts. It shall be held as special and invested for your special benefit.

In one aspect this bill may be said to place the old bank in liquidation while it at the same time creates a new one. It preserves the old body but infuses it with new life, and gives it a better assurance of continued existence. What is now needed is wisdom, courage, skill, determination. With these the Freedmen's Savings Bank may be made not only a success in itself, but a grand means of success to the colored people of the South, to whom it has already taught important lessons of industry, economy, and saving.

The history of civilization shows that no people can well rise to a high degree of mental or even moral excellence without wealth. A people uniformly poor and compelled to struggle for barely a physical existence will be dependent and despised by their neighbors, and will finally despise themselves. While it is impossible that every individual of any race shall be rich—and no man may be despised for merely being poor—yet no people can be respected which does not produce a wealthy class. Such a people will only be the hewers of wood and drawers of water, and will not rise above a mere animal existence. The mission of the Freedmen's Bank is to show our people the road to a share of the wealth and well being of the world. It has already done much to lift the race into respectability, and, with their continued confidence and patient co-operation, it will continue to reflect credit upon the race and promote their welfare.

It has long been a bitter complaint against the Freedmen's Bank that it withdrew money from distant localities and invested it here at the capital. The bill which has now become a law has removed all ground of complaint on this point. It provides that loans shall be made in the vicinity of the different branches, so that the people who deposit their money may now feel assured that it will not be withdrawn to build up Washington, but will be employed to quicken industry and improve the condition of the country where it is collected. This feature of the bill alone goes far to recommend the Freedmen's Savings and Trust Company to the confidence and favor of the colored people.

FREDERICK DOUGLASS, *President.*

(CIRCULAR NO. 2)

Washington, April 29, 1874.

TO THE EDITOR OF THE NEW YORK HERALD:

The reference in the Herald of Tuesday to the present condition of the Freedmen's Bank was not only just but considerate and generous and displays your well-known love of fair play. While that reference told the simple truth about the bank, there was nothing to produce distrust and start a run upon its deposits. Of course no banking institution in the land can well afford to invite runs upon its deposits, and it is not generous to excite such runs without good and almost irresistible necessity.

Within the last eighteen months the Freedmen's Bank, by reason of suspicions set afloat through the press and otherwise, has suffered three heavy runs upon its deposits. The last one of these, which occurred during the late financial panic, required half a million dollars to carry the bank safely through it, and the fact that it was able to survive a shock which brought other long-standing and long-trusted institutions to the ground may just now be stated, without boasting, in its favor.

The Freedmen's Bank, as its name imports, was especially established to encourage and assist the freedmen to save and increase their hard-earned money and thus to help them in the race to knowledge and higher civilization. This institution has been in existence less than ten years, and during that time it has held and handled with profit to its depositors not less than $25,000,000. The bank now comes before the public after the severest valuation of its property, rating articles at their lowest cash value in these dull times, with its liabilities $217,000 in excess of its assets. Every business man will see at once that with assets amounting, as they do, to more than $3,000,000, if only tolerably well managed and let alone, a few months only would be required to enable it to overcome this small excess of liabilities and pay all its depositors a small amount of interest.

My connection with the Freedmen's Bank as its president is of very recent date. I accepted the position with the honest purpose to forward, as well as I might, the beneficent objects had in view by its founders, to watch and guard the hard earnings of my people, and to see that those earnings shall be kept to their profit, if possible, but kept safely, at any rate.

In regard to the condition of the branches, I sent last night through the Associated Press all over the Southern States a quieting telegram, assuring our depositors that, in the opinion of the officers of the bank, if the depositors

will exercise only a reasonable degree of patience, we shall
be able to pay dollar for dollar; and this is my opinion now.

Respectfully yours,

FREDERICK DOUGLASS.

LETTER FROM FREDERICK DOUGLASS TO THE HON. A. H. GARLAND,

Reviewing Senate Bill Amending Charter of Freedmen's
Savings and Trust Company.

Washington, D. C., Feb. 19, 1880.

HON. A. H. GARLAND:

Sir: I have the honor to inform you that I have carefully read and duly considered your bill for amending the
charter of the Freedmen's Savings and Trust Company,
and for other purposes. It is in my judgment a wisely-
drawn bill. It covers the whole ground of the present situation of that institution. Its enactment by Congress would
be a credit to the national sense of justice, and would
bring speedy though small relief to a class of persons to
whom the nation cannot be too just or too generous. Many
of the newly-emancipated class put their money into this
bank, believing it to be—like the Freedmen's Bureau—a
government institution, and about as safe as the government itself. Though the misapprehension of these poor
people cannot be entirely cured by any present action of
Congress, it does appeal to Congress to exert what power
it may to help them and to restore their broken confidence.

In respect to the details of your bill, I am not sure that
you have made the commissioner's bond quite large
enough. The property is large and his power over it is
large, and while I do not attach great importance to bonds
as a guarantee of honest management, the bond in this
case should be large. I see, too, that the approval of a
majority of the trustees of the company is required in the
appointment of the commissioner. I do not know that any
positive harm can come of this feature of the bill, but I
think it an unnecessary provision of the bill. There has
been no regular meeting of the trustees as required by the
charter, this five years, and it may be fairly questioned if

today any such organization as a board of trustees of the Freedmen's Savings and Trust Company exists. If the thing can be legally done, I would for my own part prefer to have the government in *form* as well as in fact, take the assets of the defunct institution in its own hands. I believe the creditors will have nothing to lose by this absolute possession. If the clause is retained, it may cause some delay in getting the approval of the trustees, and for one I am anxious that the depositors shall get something out of this institution without delay.

Your bill recommends itself strongly in substituting *one* for *three* commissioners, for while I esteem the three present commissioners as honest and honorable men, I cannot think there is work enough to justify their retention. At the outset, when the affairs of the bank were much entangled, there may have been work for them all; but I think it is to their credit that they have in five years placed the affairs of the Freedmen's Savings and Trust Company in a condition to be easily managed by one commissioner. I have been informed that neither of the present commissioners wishes to be retained in his position, and this is well, for since there has been some want of harmony between them I am inclined to think that your bill should be so shaped that a new man shall be put in charge, and this without prejudice to either of the outgoing commissioners. It was not supposed when they were placed in charge of the Freedmen's Bank six years ago that they were to continue indefinitely. Their continuance, in part or in whole, will lead to unfriendly comments. Economy here is sufficiently strong to commend your bill at this point.

I see that you make it the duty of the Solicitor of the Treasury under the direction of the commissioner, to institute civil and criminal proceedings against trustees and managers of the bank for mismanagement and fraud. I hope this will be found unnecessary. The assets of the bank should not be further diminished by litigation from which no money can be recovered. The trustees who may be charged with mismanagement are poor, and nothing could be got out of them. Mind, however, I do not object strongly to this feature of the bill. On the score of justice, I should like to see the guilty exposed and punished; but in the interest of saving something from the wreck, I am for keeping out of the courts.

Suffice it to say in conclusion that I like your bill as a whole.

Respectfully yours,
FRED'K DOUGLASS.

5. EXTRACTS FROM THE TESTIMONY TAKEN IN 1910

In 1910 Representative Austin of Tennessee asked for a hearing before the committee on Banking and Currency in support of House Bill No. 8776 to reimburse the depositors of the Freedmen's Bank and Trust Company which had failed thirty-six years before. The members of the committee appeared to be but little interested in the matter and to know but little about the history of the bank. Among those who spoke in support of the bill were three prominent negroes: J. H. Hayes of Richmond, Virginia, lawyer and editor of *St. Luke's Herald;* Judson W. Lyons of Augusta, Georgia, formerly Register of the Treasury; and Reverend James L. White, president of the Home for Aged and Infirm Colored People, in Washington, D. C. The extracts which follow are from the statements of these men.

Statement of J. H. Hayes:

A gentleman asked the question as to the responsibility and liability of the Government, moral or legal, or what not. If you shut your eyes a minute and think of the men forty-five years ago, think of the chaos as compared to today, think of four or five millions of people turned loose, that they were free and could go among people and engage in the thrift and enterprises of the country, and there came from Washington—and everything was now at Washington, it was the Mecca then of all the Negro ideas and hopes—a mission, what were these people to think but that the Government itself had sent them to help the

Negroes? What could these four or five millions of blacks just emancipated from slavery think about that? If you will think about that, think about the fact that Congress itself had supported this movement, and that Congress had given these men authority to come in and to gather up this money and had given them the power to establish these banks, here and there, one in Richmond, and I was a depositor in that bank, and so was my father and my mother, and so were all of us there, because we thought and believed that this great big Government was behind it and that we were simply putting our funds into the hands of the Government. That is all. The Negro forty-five years ago did not have very much discretion and could not read signs. He was simply being led by the white men who had the authority and whom they believed the Government had sent, and so we turned loose every dollar we could rake and scrape and save in the hope of making something of ourselves, hoping to start out along the line of progress. . . .

I can remember that I used to walk up the bank and put in the few pennies that I could rake and scrape together. We thought that it was the Government. We did not know anything but that Congress had created it and that the United States had given the power to these people to start it. The preachers were speaking about it, and they were collecting from all the societies, churches and Sunday schools. Every cent that they could rake and scrape was shoved into this institution with the idea that in the future we were going to live more like other men. That was the condition forty-five years ago. It ran on for nine years. The Negro had no part in it, and he could not have managed it if he had. He did not have the ability or training or anything else that made it possible for him to do anything. . . .

That little failure in 1874 did more to rob the Negro of hope and to rob him of faith in banks than any other occurrence that has happened since he landed at Jamestown. . . .

Richmond was the center of all the influx of people just turned loose, and meetings were held in all the churches, and societies were being formed, and this money was collected. There was no branch at that time. The money was collected and turned over to these officers and was sent to Washington. The army officers came in and advised them to save their money, and they saved it and handed it to them, thinking that they were dealing with the Government and in dealing with the Government they were dealing with something that was strong as Gibraltar, and were simply putting the money where they could get it. Here it is right on the face of the charter. These men could not read and they would say to those people, "Here it is, 'any officer in the civil or military service of the United States.'"

Mr. Gillespie: Let us read section 7. This did not authorize the officers, civil or military, to receive deposits; it simply said if anybody wanted to make a deposit for any specific purpose that the acknowledgment of that fact might be made before a military or civil officer, and when the deposit was made it must be accompanied by this certificate. This is quite different.

Mr. Hayes: Here comes a Negro that does not know any more about getting money to Washington than he does about going to heaven. . . .

From 1865 down to 1870 the negro did not have any responsibility or vote or anything. He was the ward of the nation and hardly that. Think what that means. If there was any chancery proceeding by which the Government was responsible for these people, it certainly was responsible. They had no vote or anything. Here were the army officers of this great Government. Why did not Congress think about the fact that the Negroes were being enslaved and stop them? They had nine years. With all the information before Congress why did not somebody say: "You are involving the Government; you are making misrepresentations; you are making these people believe that this is a governmental affair when it is not."

Statement of Judson W. Lyons:

The institution was called the Freedmen's Savings and Trust Company. We all know what a trust company means. That is, we know a good deal about it, but we know that you gentlemen know all about it. We know that a trust company is something more than a bank. It implies a great deal, and the Government advised these recently emancipated people to put their money in the institution, to save it for a rainy day. They had also a Freedmen's Bureau to look after and advise us, and these people thought that this was another part of that great institution of beneficence to look after their interests. I think that is a good reason why they poured their money into that bank. The Government said that their officers might go and advise these people where to put their money, to tell them to send their receipts to Washington and the money would be deposited to their credit, and if that does not show some sort of responsibility on the part of the Government, with a view to increasing thrift and economy among those people, who were then only citizens by the emancipation proclamation, I would like to know.

Statement of Reverend James L. White:
They were told that every foot of land and every green tree in the United States was responsible and therefore it could not fail, and the colored people gathered all the money that they had earned before the war and the time of the Civil War by working at nights and Saturday afternoons and intrusted it to this bank on the recommendation of the officers of the Government.

6. LIST OF THE MOST IMPORTANT PUBLIC DOCUMENTS RELATING TO THE FREEDMEN'S BANK

House Executive Documents: No. 70, 39 Congress, 1 session; No. 144, 44 Congress, 1 session.

House Miscellaneous Documents: No. 16, 43 Congress, 2 session; No. 18, 49 Congress, 1 session; No. 34, 49 Congress, 2 session; No. 10, 48 Congress, 1 session; No. 29, 43 Congress, 2 session; No. 7, 48 Congress, 2 session; No. 34, 49 Congress, 2 session; No. 33, 51 Congress, 1 session; No. 26, 53 Congress, 2 session; No. 33, 53 Congress, 3 session.

House Documents: No. 71, 54 Congress, 2 session; No. 49, 54 Congress, 1 session; No. 97, 55 Congress, 2 session; No. 61, 55 Congress, 3 session; No. 128, 56 Congress, 1 session; No. 186, 56 Congress, 2 session; No. 83, 57 Congress, 1 session; No. 87, 57 Congress, 1 session; No. 49, 58 Congress, 2 session; No. 76, 58 Congress, 3 session; No. 185, 59 Congress, 1 session; No. 394, 59 Congress, 2 session; No. 357, 60 Congress, 1 session; No. 1176, 60 Congress, 2 session; No. 330, 61 Congress, 2 session; No. 1173, 61 Congress, 3 session; No. 1046, 62 Congress, 3 session.

House Reports: No. 502, 44 Congress, 1 session; No. 121, 41 Congress, 1 session; No. 58, 43 Congress, 2 session; No. 1991, 47 Congress, 2 session; No. 3199, 50 Congress, 1 session; No. 336, 47 Congress, 1 session; No. 1641, 55 Congress, 2 session; No. 1637, parts 1 and 2, 60 Congress, 1 session; No. 1282, parts 1 and 2, 61 Congress, 2 session.

Senate Miscellaneous Documents: No. 88, 43 Congress, 2 session; No. 10, 47 Congress, 2 session; No. 17, 47 Congress, 1 session; No. 178, 51 Congress, 1 session.

Senate Documents: No. 759, 62 Congress, 2 session.

Senate Reports: No. 440, 46 Congress, 2 session; No. 1884, 55 Congress, 3 session; No. 211, 60 Congress, 1 session; No. 434, 61 Congress, 1 and 2 sessions.

Statutes-at-Large, Volume 30, p. 1353.

Banking and Currency Committee: Hearings in January, 1910, on House Bill 8776 to reimburse depositors of the Freedmen's Savings and Trust Company. 23 pages. Not printed in the public documents of the House or Senate.

INDEX

Alabama, deposits in branch banks, 49; cashier short in accounts, 62, 66.

Allotment System for Negro soldiers, 9.

Alvord, John W., plans savings bank for Negroes, 23, 24; corresponding secretary, 32; inspector of Freedmen's Bureau Schools, 32; vice-president of Freedmen's Savings Bank, 32; travels in the South, 34; established branch banks, 47; president of the bank, 39, 68, 110; loses influence, 69; is not reelected, 74, 85; opposes investigation by Congress, 83; president of the Seneca Sandstone Company, 86.

Amendment of Freedmen's Savings Bank charter in 1870, 136.

American Building Block Company, interest in bank, 40, 68.

Anderson, Rev. D. W., vice-president of the bank, 39.

Atlanta, Georgia, branch bank, cashier short in accounts, 61.

Augusta, Georgia, branch bank, 50.

Austin, representative from Tennessee, introduces bill to pay depositors, 128, 159.

Balloch, Gen. G. W., of Freedmen's Bureau, gives office space to branches of Freedmen's Savings Bank, 36; a trustee of the bank, 39, 68, 76, 77, 110.

Baltimore branch bank, 50.

Banks, Gen. N. P., establishes "Free Labor Bureau" in Louisiana, 7; organizes "Free Labor Bank," 20.

Beaufort, S. C., military savings bank established, 21; absorbed by Freedmen's Savings Bank, 33; local board of branch bank, 43; does regular banking business, 43; has specific privileges, 62; whites make use of bank, 63; shortage at branch bank, 63.

Beecher, Edwin, cashier at Montgomery, short in accounts, 62, 66.

Black Codes, laws passed in 1865–1866 by Southern legislatures, 13.

Bliss, of New York, member of Douglas committee, 108.

Booth, William A., first president of Freedmen's Savings Bank, 32.

Border States, slavery destroyed in, 4.

Boston, assistant cashier in Washington bank, 63.

Boyle, Juan, curious transaction with the bank, 97.

Bradford, member of Congress from Alabama, on Freedmen's Savings Bank, 41, 112; member of Douglas committee, 108.

Branch Banks, best of, 38; not all pay expenses, 54; shortages, 66.

Brawley, estimate of Freedmen's Savings Bank, 129.

Bronough, cashier at Vicksburg branch, short in accounts, 66.

Bruce, B. K., Senator from Mississippi; chairman of Senate committee to investigate the Freedmen's Savings Bank, 108.

Bruce committee, membership, 108; report, 112.

Buckalew, senator from Pennsylvania, on Freedmen's Savings Bank Bill, 25.

Butler, Gen. B. F., frees Negroes at Fortress Monroe, 6; establishes his military savings bank at Norfolk, 21; "Free Labor Bureau" in Louisiana, 7.